The Book
of Rosy

The Book of Rosy

A MOTHER'S STORY OF SEPARATION AT THE BORDER

Rosayra Pablo Cruz
and Julie Schwietert Collazo

HarperOne
An Imprint of HarperCollins*Publishers*

HarperOne

HarperCollins books may be purchased for educational, business, or sales promotional use. For information, please email the Special Markets Department at SPsales@harpercollins.com.

FIRST EDITION

Designed by Yvonne Chan

Library of Congress Cataloging-in-Publication Data

Names: Pablo Cruz, Rosayra, author. | Schwietert Collazo, Julie, author.
Title: The book of Rosy : a mother's story of separation at the border / Rosayra Pablo Cruz and Julie Schwietert Collazo.
Description: First edition. | New York, NY : HarperOne, 2020.
Identifiers: LCCN 2019050658 (print) | LCCN 2019050659 (ebook) | ISBN 9780062941923 (hardcover) | ISBN 9780062941947 (ebook)
Subjects: LCSH: Pablo Cruz, Rosayra. | Schwietert Collazo, Julie. | Illegal alien children—Government policy—United States. | Illegal aliens—Government policy—United States. | Juvenile detention—United States. | Deportation—United States. | Mother and child. | Guatemalans—Legal status, laws, etc. — United States. | Mothers—Guatemala—Biography.
Classification: LCC JV6600 .P34 2020 (print) | LCC JV6600 (ebook) | DDC 362.87092 [B] —dc23
LC record available at https://lccn.loc.gov/2019050658
LC ebook record available at https://lccn.loc.gov/2019050659

---

20 21 22 23 24 LSC 10 9 8 7 6 5 4 3 2 1

Contents

PART I

1. The Visit   3

2. Doors   19

3. Hunger   37

4. The Migrant Highway   53

5. Trucks   69

6. Arrival   95

7. The Icebox   101

8. Separation   107

9. Lockup   111

10. Takeoff and Landing   125

11. Reunion   135

PART II

12. A Wild Idea   143

13. Rebuilding a Family   181

Contents

PART III

14. Bittersweet Season   *191*

15. School Days   *201*

16. The Horizon   *205*

Epilogue   *217*

Recommended Reading   *231*

How to Get Involved   *235*

Acknowledgments—Rosy   *239*

Acknowledgments—Julie   *243*

PART
I

1

The Visit

Rosayra Pablo Cruz.

When said with love, my first name rolls off the tongue, the trilled *r*'s cascading over so many soft vowels, like Guatemala's crystal clear Río Azul rippling over smooth stones. But the guard's voice is brusque and gruff, bothered. It isn't her job to love, nor to even think about the first names of the detainees being held in their cells here at the Eloy Detention Center in Arizona. We are last names only. We are numbers. Nine numbers, in fact, which, when punched into immigration's online database, can tell you who someone is and where and when they were born.

What it can't tell you is that thirty-five years ago and more than two thousand miles away, my mother, Fernanda Cruz Pablo, labored at home for nearly twelve hours, at least half of those in a darkness punctured only by the flickering light of a fire made with branches of ocote, an evergreen that gives up its piney fragrance when burned. Refugio, one of our town's midwives, sat by her side and prepared my mother for the final push. As I was born, my mother sent up a prayer that God would bless and keep me, and that He might, if she could be so bold to ask, even make my life a little bit easier than hers had been so far.

The guard calls my name again, with even more roughness in her voice.

PABLO CRUZ. VISIT.

I stir from the bottom bunk in my cramped cell, glancing at her in disbelief. I demur and shake my head. No, I can't possibly have a visitor. I don't know anyone in Arizona. I haven't taken the advice of fellow detainees to reach out to an attorney who might be able to help me, not even after my cell mate spent her own commissary money on a phone call to my family in Guatemala, urging them to persuade me to call the lawyer. "Rosayra," she whispered to me, "at least *call* him. See if he can help you! What do you have to lose?"

Why bother? I thought, repeating the question to my oldest sister, Elvira, when we managed to speak on the phone. I have no money to pay for a lawyer, and neither does my family. In fact, we have all taken on debt for me to be able to come to the United States with my sons, and we are all under pressure to pay it off quickly, with interest. The sooner I can get out of here, the sooner I can be with my sons, file for asylum, and get a work authorization permit. Once I have that permit, I can earn some money, pay off my debts, and make sure my family is taken care of. The process won't be fast, I know, but every day that I am in here is a day that I cause my family stress, as they worry about what I owe. Every day that I am in here is a day that puts them at risk, for unpaid debts can mean a death sentence in my country.

This is the reality for nearly every migrant from Central America who flees to the United States. Almost no one has money to make the journey on their own, so they borrow it from people who do. Then, they are bound to the obligation of repaying it, usually thousands of dollars, with interest. You can't possibly understand how fast interest accrues until you've made one of these deals and lived with the anxiety of meeting the payment deadlines.

Let's GO, Pablo Cruz!

La Miss, the name we use for all of the guards, is getting really annoyed now.

This must be a mistake. The idea that someone would have traveled to this dusty desert town and its for-profit immigration prison just to see me is inconceivable.

But La Miss insists. Perhaps the visitor is one of the kind-faced volunteers from the Casa Mariposa Detention Visitation Program. They have never come to see me specifically, but the volunteers write letters to detained women and come for weekly visits, a much-needed reminder that at least a handful of people outside the walls and the barbed wire know and care about what is happening inside.

I shuffle out of my cell in my detention center–issued canvas tennis shoes, which slap the floor, flapping uselessly like a pair of broken bird wings. One shoe is lighter in color than the other, worn out from use on the many feet that have been in them before mine. Nothing is new here; everything is used, each item an archive of stories and the pain of the people who have preceded us.

Neither shoe has laces. The only shoes that have laces at Eloy are the guards' boots. Laces are weapons; they can be used to harm another detainee, to choke the breath out of her, or—and there are whispered stories about this—to hang oneself if desperation cuts that deep. These stories don't surprise me. In my short time here, I have seen women go crazy with hysteria. They curl up on their bunks and refuse to leave their cells. They cry without ceasing, as if their bodies are bottomless wells of tears. I have seen them shut down, becoming shells of who they once were. I have seen them lose their will to fight, their will to go on. It's terrifying to witness how quickly this can happen, terrifying to see that nothing you can say or do has the power to bring them back from the edge of their own wildness.

That wildness, that savage wilderness . . . I can feel its dark perimeter, too, as if it's moving in from the periphery of my own being. It's like standing in a vast cornfield and watching a storm gather strength, its furious clouds whipping themselves into ever-larger ones, their size and speed doubling suddenly in front of your eyes, before they release a lashing rain that races across the field toward you. But the darkness inside myself I try to push back, using my will to hold it at bay. Early on here, I realized that surviving detention would require mental and emotional control. I'm not numb, but I don't want to cry. If I start, I might not stop. I ache for my two boys, of course, but if I let my tears flow, I will become one of those women, hanging on the edge of her own being, and then, what will I be able to do to get my boys, who have been taken from me, back into my arms?

In the visitation room, I scan the faces but don't recognize any of them, so I wait for La Miss to indicate my visitor. She jabs her finger in the air, pointing to a tall, thin man, who is dressed in a nice suit and wears a stylish straw hat. He looks Latino, and later, I'll learn that he's an immigrant, too; he is from Nicaragua. He's thumbing through a somewhat disorganized sheaf of papers in front of him. "You wanted to see me?" I ask.

"Your name?" he replies.

"Rosayra Pablo Cruz."

"Pablo Cruz, Pablo Cruz, Pablo Cruz." He looks up from the papers. "No, I'm sorry, you're not on my list."

I look at him in confusion. "I'm not sure, but they told me to come see you," I explain.

"Come," he says, gesturing toward a chair. "Sit. Let's talk."

José Orochena introduces himself. He explains that he is a New York City attorney working with a group of activist mothers in New York who have raised large amounts of money to post bond for mothers like me, who have been separated from their children at the border because of a policy called "zero tolerance." The moms started raising money on June 25, he explains, and they had planned to post bond for only one mother. But so many Americans are so angry about this policy that the moms have raised enough money to post bond for more women. He explains that the zero-tolerance policy was intended to discourage those of us fleeing violence in Central America from seeking asylum in the United States. It was put into effect on April 6, 2018. I crossed the Mexico-US border with my sons ten days later, on April 16. Had we arrived just eleven days earlier, our story would be very different from the one I am telling here.

None of us detained in Eloy ever knew about this policy before we set out on our journeys. Word of it never reached our towns and villages. Nightly news, for those of us who have televisions, tends to focus on local happenings: the latest gang-inflicted, extortion-related death; or a gruesome highway accident, with video showing the horrifying moment of impact over and over again as a commentator prattles on as if narrating an exciting sports event. For those of us who fled our home countries during the zero-tolerance period, we arrived at the border with hope—some of us having tried to cross before or, like me, having done so successfully—only to have our children taken away from us without warning. Many of the women imprisoned here didn't even get to say goodbye to their children.

Had we known about the policy, would we have made a different decision? I don't know. It's impossible to say. How does a person choose one danger over another?

José tells me more about the moms and the first woman they got out of Eloy. They paid her $7,500 bond and brought her from Arizona to New York, where her children were in foster care. Her children were at a place called Cayuga Centers, which is where my boys are, too. Within a week, the activist moms had freed several more mothers who had been separated from their children by the zero-tolerance policy—Amalia, Irma, all beautiful names. José is not an immigration attorney, but I don't know this right now; there isn't time for him to explain that to me. He has other women to see during his quick visit to Eloy today. It's July 9. Since he and the activist moms freed Yeni González García on June 28, his phone has been ringing off the hook, with calls coming in at all hours of the day and night. He says the activist moms are "public enemy number one at Eloy" because they've given hope to those of us who are detained here.

That hope takes the form of ten digits: José's cell phone number. Before she was released, Yeni had shared José's number with other detainees, and it had been copied time and again, circulating around the detention center faster than a juicy rumor. Women call him when they can get phone time, if they're lucky enough to have someone who can deposit money into an account that allows them to make calls to the outside world. The connection is often bad, with static crackling on the line or a delay causing unnatural jumps and starts in the conversation. The lines to make the calls are long, and the money runs out fast because the calls are expensive, but hope and the desire to connect are stubborn and patient.

José has become something of a folk hero among many detainees; when Yeni was released, the facility was put on lockdown so the rest of us wouldn't know someone was being freed, but word spread. The women who had heard about him, the ones who had had his phone number pressed into their hands by another detainee, hoped they'd be the next ones to walk out of Eloy's gates and leave this hell behind.

In addition to giving out José's phone number, Yeni had done something else. She had memorized vast amounts of information about the women with whom she spent time in detention, and she provided José with a list of mothers who could use his help. He was astonished by her recall, how she stored all of these details about so many other women and their children. But my name wasn't on this list, and I had never called him. In fact, I had never even known his name. The number circulating around Eloy was just identified as belonging to *El Abogado*, the lawyer, and since I didn't have money, I'd been hardheaded and didn't even want to call him.

These facts only reinforce my sense that something of the divine is at work here. The papers and folders José carries have the names of the mothers from Yeni's list, as well as the ones who have called him. I don't fall into either category, so how have we been connected, if not by God's own hand? Alongside their names, he has added notations about their countries of origin and the names, ages, and locations of their children, and he is trying to put all the information together like a dot-to-dot picture, which will yield a coherent, cohesive image if he just follows the right sequence.

Do I have a bond offer? he asks. I do: $12,000. It is an impossible sum, and one whose calculation seems arbitrary. Where are my children? New York City. What are their names? Yordy and Fernando. Their ages? Fifteen and five. What is my nine-digit alien number, or A-number? He scribbles my answers on a piece of scrap paper. As soon as he leaves the facility, he will text Julie, the woman who is in charge of the New York moms, and ask whether they have raised enough money to pay for my freedom. He feels certain they have. As he stands up and pushes his chair back, he says something that sounds like an improbable promise. "You'll be released soon," he assures me. He shakes my hand and says he'll be in touch.

I am incredulous, certain that this friendly, seemingly well-meaning man has made a grave error. What kind of people would pay a $12,000 bond for someone they have never met and know nothing about? How do they even come up with that kind of money? As I walk back to my cell, I am overcome by confusion, but I allow myself a tiny spark of hope. After all, I have been begging God for a sign.

―――――

When I first arrived at the Eloy Detention Center, I joined a number of the detained women in the yard, where we'd spend our two hours of daily outdoor recreation time in communal prayer. We continue to meet now, dressed in drab green prison uniforms that conceal the used and soiled undergarments we were given upon our admission to Eloy. We pray for obvious things, such as the patience to make it through day after day of utter tedium, and the strength to bear the insufferable conditions in the detention center: the inadequate and often spoiled food; the thin mattresses and tightly rationed toiletries; the water that seems to be laden with chemicals, leaving many women's hands, including my own, peeled and red, as if burned; the inability to discern what day it is; the insensitive response to every medical request, however severe ("Take an ibuprofen and drink more water"); and, the worst, the unfathomable cruelty of some of the guards—all women—many of whom speak Spanish fluently but refuse to communicate with us in any language but English.

To many of the detainees, it seems that the guards enjoy tormenting us, yelling and threatening disciplinary action, including solitary confinement, for infractions like hugging one another, braiding another woman's hair, or hiding a piece of bread in one's bra to be eaten when hunger strikes late at night. The guards are women who can't seem to entertain the thought of being in our place, and so they treat us as lesser humans, making us beg for an extra sanitary napkin, for instance, or telling us over and over again that the suffering we are experiencing now is something we brought upon ourselves. Even though they seem so heartless, we pray for them, too, asking God to forgive them for their sins and lead them to a place of understanding.

But most of all, the women in the prayer circle take turns offering petitions for their children: "God, please keep our children safe, wherever they are." "God, please touch our children's hearts, and let them know we haven't abandoned them." "God, I beg you, please reunite us with our children soon." Hot, salty tears roll down most women's cheeks, and we do our best to console each other without doing something that would put us in solitary confinement, or "the hole," for a disciplinary infraction.

Our voices falter, small sounds in a vast, open, grassless space that is baked by the searing southwestern sun. We are closed in by chain-link fences and barbed wire. Though we are outside, the outside world feels distant.

A *compañera* walked the fence's interior perimeter recently, trying to determine whether it would be feasible to hold a protest, to try to make people aware that we are here, to tell them what's happening inside Eloy. When she reported back to the others who were interested, her voice was heavy with disappointment. "We are far from anything," she said. "I saw no people, no cars. We are in the middle of nowhere." Later, I'll learn that many detention centers operated under contract with the US Immigration and Customs Enforcement (ICE) are in similar places, far from towns, outside the sight of ordinary US citizens.

The isolation, the desolation . . . this is why the prayer circles are sustenance, a ray of light and a breath of hope in an otherwise dark and airless existence inside Eloy. If my own prayers are not sufficient—and I'd begun having some doubts that they were effective—I feel certain the collective invocations of so many mothers could reach God's ears and touch His heart.

But by the end of June, more than two months into my detention, I was no longer so sure that God would grant my request for release from the literal and psychological prison in which I found myself trapped with so many other desperate mothers. My prayers changed. In April and May, I had prayed to be reunited with my sons. The fact that my prayer went unanswered suggested to me that maybe I needed to ask for something different.

Perhaps I needed to release my desire to be with my boys—maybe it was selfish. If God had a reason for me to remain imprisoned in Eloy, He would make it clear in due course. So, I began to center my prayers around what I believed my boys needed. "Please God," I begged, as I lay in my bunk at night, struggling to fall asleep, "make sure my sons are with someone who will take care of them as if they were her own."

I have been reading a book called *The Key to Your Expected End.* The author, Katie Souza, is someone who has been in prison, too, and her words touch me deeply. She experienced a transformation: prison changed her life. It made her a better person. As I read her words, the thought occurs to me that while I wouldn't have chosen this place for myself, maybe I am at Eloy Detention Center for a reason. God has my full attention, no distractions, and He can mold me. Prison—and Eloy Detention Center *is* a prison—is not a beautiful experience. It's certainly not a five-star hotel. There's no privacy, not even when you go to the bathroom. Early on, you negotiate with your cell mate: you turn your back when I need to use the toilet, and I'll do the same for you. Prison is a difficult place to be. But it strips you down to your most essential self, and things can happen to you here that make you a better person. God is at work here.

Once I realized this, once my prayers changed, something shifted; I could feel it. I began having vivid dreams, dreams so powerful and real that they left me drained and disoriented, wondering whether I was asleep or awake. The one that rattled me the most occurred on the morning of June 26, just after breakfast.

Our days have a predictable, monotonous cadence. Guards wake us up at 4:30 a.m., and we line up for breakfast at 5. Following the always-rushed meal of a cold, hard-boiled egg and bland oatmeal, foods that sink to the pit of your stomach and sit there for hours, we are herded back to our cells by 6 a.m., locked back in while we await one of several daily counts. I lie down on my bunk, trying, unsuccessfully, to find a comfortable spot. The thin mattress spread across the metal bed frame never offers rest or relief, and the air conditioning blows unrelentingly, directly onto the bottom bed. I always cover the vent with an old shirt—the thin blankets we are given aren't enough to keep any of us warm—but it doesn't help much; I shiver and hug myself as tightly as I can.

There is little to do during lockdown and count, and I was tired that day, so I soon fell asleep. Almost immediately, I began to dream. I am at a prayer service, standing up, and I begin to speak my prayer: "God guide me in my path, and give me the wisdom to know that I am doing the right thing." Suddenly, a voice says, "Read Matthew 6:4–30."

"Who's interrupting the service?" I ask in annoyance. But when I turn around to identify the offender, I discover that no one has said a word.

The voice speaks again, insistent: "Read Matthew 6:4–30." In the dream, I look for something to write with, so I can make note of the verses—and at that same moment, I woke up.

I believe in the power of dreams. My mother has had many prophetic dreams in her life, dreams in which messages are conveyed to her. Through dreams, she has received answers to her dilemmas or solutions to her problems. Such dreams have guided many of her decisions. The same is true for me. Perhaps our lives are braided together even more tightly than I realize.

Although I wasn't sure whether I was awake or still in a dream state, I found my Bible. The verses in Matthew seemed illuminated, as if they were a message meant expressly for me. They address many of our greatest human dilemmas, including the acts of faith we perform in public, for approval, versus those we perform in private, those that are meant wholly and exclusively for God and His glorification. The verses also speak of forgiveness, of pardoning those who have offended us so that we, too, might be forgiven by God. They talk about the treasures of earth and the treasures of heaven, and about our eyes as the light of our bodies, the lanterns of our souls. They talk about God and riches, and they remind us of the fact that no one can serve two gods. They speak of those believers who possess great faith and those of little faith, and they seem to pose the questions, "Which kind of believer are you?" "When you make an offering, are you asking for something at the same time?" "Does your right hand know what your left hand is doing?"

I made notes alongside the verses, using a dull pencil to draw asterisks and other symbols, like eyelashes, to remind me that these are the words toward which I should direct my attention. Then, I turned to the back of the Bible, where there are blank pages for notes, and I wrote the dream down. I knew immediately what I had to do. I had to let go. I had to be a believer who has great faith. I had to be someone who gives without asking. I had to surrender fully to God, to stop asking for what *I* want. I had to say, simply, "God, let *Thy* will be done."

And that was the exact moment when things began moving in my favor. I felt a lightness overcome my body and my being, and I experienced a peace unlike anything I had felt in ages, maybe ever, and certainly for the first time since I had been detained at Eloy.

The dream set things into motion. José Orochena visits me on July 9, 2018. Two days later, the gates of Eloy swing open, and I step into the arid Arizona air, squinting in the shimmering heat.

2

Doors

It definitely wasn't the first time I'd asked God for a sign. In my constant conversations with God, I have frequently asked Him to show me the door. I would walk through it with trust and in faith. I just needed to see it.

Sometimes, the door was literal. That was the case in 2014, when I had come to the United States for the first time.

After my husband, Juan Alberto, was murdered in 2008, I felt a cloud of fear creeping across the horizon of my life. Yordy, my oldest child, was just six, and I was at a loss to explain to him how and why his father had been killed. No words are adequate to make sense of such a gaping hole blown into the middle of somcone's life, especially when that person is a child.

At first, I held the news of Juan Alberto's death to myself. I got the call early in the morning. We didn't live together at the time, but he always called me at 6 a.m., and when the phone rang, I was certain it was him. I noticed, though, that the number was different; it was my mother-in-law's number. I answered tentatively.

"They killed Juanito, my child," she said, in a voice I will never forget as long as I live.

"What? How? Who?" I wanted to scream, but I held myself back, so as not to terrify Yordy and his younger sister, Dulce, who was just two, out of their sweet dreams.

I woke the kids up gently and took a combi bus to Huehue-tenango, where my mother-in-law lived. I was a mess, crying uncontrollably, and I happened to run into a woman along the way who had been a close friend of Juan Alberto's and who loved him very much. "What's wrong, Rosy?" she asked, fearing my answer. In Guatemala, almost everyone has lost someone they love to murder. We are a nation whose ghosts hover in the air around us, a country of walking dead.

"Juan Alberto is gone," I replied, unable to stop the flow of tears. She bought me water and tried to console me, but it was no use. My sister called and asked where I was. I told her I wasn't home, but I didn't want to share the news with my family yet. Word travels fast in Guatemala, though, and some of my siblings soon showed up at my mother-in-law's house, too.

Juan Alberto's funeral was a strange fever dream, so different from any other funeral I'd ever attended. His family had decided that he would be buried in a different town, and so we all had to make a long journey, several hours, to get there. In our home-town, when you attend a funeral, everyone—even the poorest person—brings flowers, and you lay them on the coffin or the tomb. In our town's cemetery, the coffin is laid upon a concrete stand before it is buried. The cemetery's entrance gate leads to a concrete walkway, and everyone processes down the sidewalk with their flowers. They come to a stop at the coffin, which is shielded from the sun and rain by a tin roof, and they lay the flowers down, as candles flicker on the ground at their feet. They cry and touch the coffin and hold vigil until the burial.

When we arrived in the town where Juan Alberto's funeral was taking place, I saw no flowers: no one carried a bouquet or a single stem, except me, and I saw none in the cemetery, either. Instead, there was an enormous pile of sacks. Some were filled with corn, others with sugar—sacks and sacks and sacks, all heaped into a mountainous mound. Next to the towering sacks was a trio of gigantic clay pots, as wide as your arms can make a circle, and as deep as your hips are tall. One had rice in it, and another, tamales. I don't remember what the third one contained. Everyone was eating—at the funeral! After they finished stuffing themselves, people gathered up as much food as they could, scooping leftovers into plastic bags to carry home with them. *This is really the strangest thing*, I thought, struggling to make sense of it all.

So many people were there, and truly, I didn't know a soul! I also didn't know at the time that this town's tradition—so different from my town's traditions—was for *everyone* to attend every funeral, even if they had never met the deceased. Yordy looked at the throngs of townspeople in attendance and marveled at their tear-soaked faces. He wanted to cry himself, but the tears were stubborn and wouldn't come. Why, he wondered, were so many people who didn't even know his father, who had never gone horseback riding with him or had never bounced on his knee or felt the pleasant roughness of his hand on their head, crying as if they had lost someone dear to them, someone they loved completely?

I didn't know how to answer his questions. For one thing, the presence of so many strangers was as odd for me as it was for him. For another, I was distraught, distracted by my family's ballooning needs and the fact that Juan Alberto's death made me the head of household and sole provider, just as had been the case with my own mother. I watched my husband's remains be put to rest inside a niche marked only by his initials, J.A.M.V. We couldn't afford for his entire name to be chiseled out on the stone. One day, I hope I can return to the town to replace the concrete slab with one that is etched with his entire name. I hope I can stand there and touch my hand to the stone and tell him about my years without him, what our children and I have suffered, but also, what we have become.

I had little time to mourn. I was seven months pregnant with my youngest daughter, Britny, and I'd have a lot more to do than answer questions and comfort my children if I didn't get back to work quickly. I bid Juan Alberto a final goodbye and made the long journey back to San Antonio Huista.

The days that followed were the darkest ones I had ever experienced. I was inconsolable, falling into a deep depression. I didn't want to take care of myself. I didn't want to get dressed up or put on makeup, as I had before his death. I had always taken pride in my appearance and I liked to look nice, but now, I could barely stir from my bed to brush my hair or my teeth.

I cooked for my kids and made sure they were cared for, but the energy this required was all that I could muster. After I fed the kids their dinner, I'd go outside and walk around the house and find a place out there to cry, where no one could see me. My family and I were close, but I tried to keep them at arm's length, avoiding their questions and their consolations. If anyone could have understood what I was going through, it was my mother, who had also lost her husband at such a young age and had had children, including me, who were around the same age as my children. My mother tried to talk with me, asking gently, "*Mi hija*, how are you?" but I couldn't even speak with her, my closest confidant. I was mired so deep in my pain.

Sometime after Juan Alberto was killed, I started drinking. I had never had a drinking problem, but now, I felt like I *needed* beer or tequila. A big hole had opened up inside of me, and I was trying to fill that emptiness with alcohol. I'd get drunk, and then feel guilty. I felt such disgust that my children saw me like that. *How stupid!* I thought, judging myself harshly but unable to change my behavior. I knew my children were trying to survive, trying to overcome the death of their father, and there I was, wasted and falling apart. "I'm fine, I'm fine; don't worry about me," I'd say to them as they looked at me with worry and fear. But the truth is, I was broken and had no idea how to put myself back together. I'd try to sleep but I couldn't. My mind was like a computer processing large amounts of information. I wanted to turn it off. But you can't turn the human mind off. It doesn't work that way.

Maybe it sounds strange—it sounds odd to me, too—but even though ours wasn't the best relationship, I felt like half of me died when Juan Alberto was killed. In part, that's because I had come to understand that he acted the way he did—possessive, controlling—because he had been hurt and poisoned by his experiences, too, as so many people are in their lives. I look at a photo of us that was taken before his death and I see how much pain we are carrying, how much ownership he felt over me, by the way his arm is wrapped tightly around my chest. I try not to, but I can't help but think about what might have been. What could we have become together? What kind of life could we have built for our children? How might we have healed each other's hurts, if we had just had more time together?

Despite our problems, I had loved him deeply. His death hurt me so much, and it left me with feelings I had never experienced before. I felt hate, a black, all-consuming rage toward whoever had killed him. I thought to myself, *If I knew who killed him, I would kill them with my own two hands*. I even contemplated suicide. But I wondered what would happen to my children, to Yordy, Dulce, and our baby, Britny. She was born after his death, so Juan Alberto would never have the chance to know her. My children hadn't done anything to deserve losing one parent, let alone two if I were to take my own life. In fact, the greatest source of my pain in response to Juan Alberto's death was my awareness that our children would grow up without knowing the feel of a father's embrace. I had known that myself. I could easily recall what it felt like to see a friend's father give her a hug and wonder, *What does that feel like? I'd like to know. I'd like to have my father.*

The weeks and months following Juan Alberto's death were a horrible time. We filed a police report, but they didn't want to investigate. To tell you the truth, I didn't want them to investigate, either. I was afraid that whoever had killed him would kill me and our children, too. That's common in Guatemala. Sometimes, I imagine the insides of every police precinct in this country, and I envision stacks and stacks of file folders containing reports of so many deaths, each one a chronicle of pain that will never be assuaged. And almost none of us demand otherwise; we are terrified of exposing our families to more danger. I was, too.

We never learned who killed Juan Alberto. We never had closure. We had to simply ask God for help, to give us the strength to go on. And me? I had to get back to work.

In a way, I was lucky, because I had a job, and so many people didn't. Unemployment is a massive problem in my country. Even well-off people who go to school and earn a degree discover that it is difficult, if not impossible, to find a decent, good-paying job. If you find one, it's probably because you already have money or connections. My family has never had either of these. My mother has never stepped foot in a school, and she can't read. She never knew "important" people, never had connections that could smooth the way for her or for us. She earned a meager living and gained respect by always working hard, whether that meant living in someone's home and working as their servant, cleaning the house, doing the laundry, and making tortillas, or, later, buying goods wholesale, like beans, and reselling them in the local market.

Over years and years of working for a pittance, she was able to save up enough to establish her own *comedor*, a food stand in the town's market. Now in her late sixties, she still shows up there every day, teaching one or another of my nieces or cousins how to make perfect tortillas, or how to make the rich broth that forms the base of Guatemala's beloved chicken soup. She always wears an apron around her waist, her hands dipping in and out of the apron's pockets to make change for customers who buy fruit or vegetables from her display in front of the *comedor*. From my mother, we all learned how to strive to do better, to survive, to respect other people, to have values. She has been my best example, my inspiration.

My own schooling had been limited, but I had an entrepreneurial streak and I was a hard worker. Before Juan Alberto's death, I had been determined to build a stable life for our family. I managed to take out a loan and secure my own storefront on credit. There, I sold women's clothing and accessories. To anyone else's eye, it seemed like fine work, and easy enough, too, just standing behind a counter all day and waiting for customers. But after his death, because of my depression, I was exhausted, running on fumes. I knew what it took to run a successful business in a small town, and I was an exacting entrepreneur. I'd get up long before dawn to load my goods, roll the metal gate up on the shop's storefront, and spend the next few hours arranging all the wares just so. Competition was relentless and fierce. More than 59 percent of Guatemalans live below the poverty line, so there's no such thing as disposable income. Shopkeepers are always battling for a limited number of quetzales. The way to stand out and persuade customers to spend their money with me was by styling the most attractive displays; always ensuring varied and fresh inventory; making sure that I could outlast everyone else, opening earlier and closing later; and maintaining consistent hours of operation.

That kind of dedication leads to success, however modest it might be. But it also exacts a cost. In Central America, business owners are frequently the targets of criminal gangs, whose members use extortion to wring more money out of the legitimate economy so they can funnel it into the underground economy. They impose a "protection tax" on businesses: pay *us*, they say, and we'll make sure you don't have any problems. This tax isn't elective; opt out and the price will likely be continuous harassment or even death, not just for business owners, but for their families, too. This criminal system has put many shops out of business. It has even resulted in the deaths of far more modest vendors, like a forty-eight-year-old woman who made tortillas and sold them from a homemade wooden stand she set up on a sidewalk in the town of Escuintla. She barely made a living, so she had no money to pay the tax. She was killed brutally—shot and left on the sidewalk to die—when she refused to pay up.

Three years after Juan Alberto was killed, I narrowly escaped death myself. One evening in 2011, while walking home around dusk, I took a shortcut through an alleyway. I saw my would-be murderer at the other end of the alley and thought nothing of him at first—a young man wearing a ball cap, hanging out, as young men do. Several of the houses in this part of the neighborhood rented out rooms to students; maybe he was one of them. There was no reason to be afraid. It was only when I saw him pull the brim of his cap down, as if to cover his eyes, that my skin started to prickle with worry about his presence, his motives. Before I could think more about the scenario, he had pulled out his gun and fired.

The first bullet went through my left wrist. I had been going home from my mother's food stall at the town's market and was carrying a bucket. I dropped the bucket and instinctively threw my arms up in an X formation, as if I could protect my face and my chest with them, as if I could ward off more bullets. The second bullet went through one side of my right wrist, exiting the other side. I screamed, of course, and cried out for help. I turned and ran, stumbling, out of the alley, ducking into the open door of a house and begging the owner to help me. The shooter fled.

Blood flowed from the wounds. My right arm was like a flower blown open, the skin splayed like petals in that brief moment between full maturity and wilting death, its innards exposed completely. The color crimson blossomed on my clothes, rivulets flowing even into my underwear, leaving a trail behind me. When volunteer firefighters arrived and I was carried to an ambulance, I heard a nurse ask whether I had my period. I felt like I was floating above the scene, and I couldn't speak, but an onlooker retorted, "How could you ask her that? Can't you see that she's covered in blood? She was shot! SHOT! That's not her period!" The minutes stretched out into what seemed like eternity, blood seeping down my legs and pooling in my shoes. Firefighters cut my pants off with a pair of scissors. They tugged on my shoes, pulling them off and throwing them aside. I remember clearly that the shoes were purple.

———

I didn't think I had enemies, but it was obvious that someone wanted me dead. Word filtered down to me, as it always does in a small town: perhaps it was an ex-girlfriend of my boyfriend, Nery, who was jealous and wanted me out of the picture. We'd started dating in late 2010, just enough time for envy and resentment to wear on the heart and mind of someone else who thought that she loved him and hoped that he loved her, someone who thought she could tame him and make him hers, who could turn him into a one-woman kind of man. Talk on the street was that the ex had paid a hit man to take me out. Could that really be the case? I wasn't sure, but it sounded like a reasonable possibility.

The crime certainly wasn't random. Without question, the man who shot me knew my schedule. He was aware of my comings and goings. He knew I'd be passing by that exact place, around that exact time, coming from the market, where I helped my mother close up in the evenings. He knew where we lived, and he knew that the path to our home was a prime place to kill: like a favela in Brazil, houses were staggered on a hill, arranged along a single concrete-paved path that climbed straight up. There was no exit at the top, and our home was the last one on the path—no escape. In a small town like ours, it's not hard at all to figure out people's habits and to take advantage of their routines in order to do them harm. Small towns make violence and extortion easy. The geography of poverty makes them even easier.

Regardless of the shooter's motive or who gave him the instructions to take my life and paid him to try to do so, the shooting was a wake-up call for me. How could it be otherwise? As early as the second shot, the one that passed through my right wrist, I was in conversation with God. "God, if I die right now, where will my soul go? Please have mercy on me," I begged. I knew that my relationship with Nery was a problem. Nery, who was a ladies' man and more than twenty years older than me, was also still married. In 2012, when I was pregnant with our son, Fernando, I learned that his wife was also pregnant. Eventually, it would dawn on me that our relationship couldn't be called anything other than what it was: adultery.

As I was bleeding onto the concrete floor of a neighbor's house, waiting for help, I asked God to give me a chance to fix my life and allow me to live without sin. "Have mercy, Lord," I whispered as I labored to breathe. That was the word—

MERCY—that saved me. I know that in my heart. God allowed me to live so that I could correct my ways and fulfill my promise.

It would take a couple of years before I extracted myself from that relationship, but God was patient. He gave me that chance.

————

My brother, Delfino, rode with me in the ambulance. He's always the first person to show up, despite his own problems—and he has a lot of them. At the hospital, which is more than an hour away from our home, my wounds were cleaned and I was stitched up without anesthetic, which hurt every bit as much as you might imagine it would. The next day, I was transferred to a clinic closer to home, where doctors performed surgery on both of my arms. The scars will be there forever, reminding me of a terrible mystery that will never be solved. As with Juan Alberto's murder, we reported the attempt on my life to the police. The report, which I saw later, was full of errors, a worthless accounting of what had happened that would never lead to the criminal's capture or conviction.

When I returned to my hometown, I had to walk around holding my head high, acting as if I wasn't afraid, even though I had so much fear inside. I couldn't show it because I didn't want my mother to be more scared than she already was. I didn't want my children to be afraid, either. And I didn't want to seem vulnerable to anyone who might do us harm. Since the person who had wanted to kill me had failed in their attempt, there was always the possibility that they might try again. I had to show that I was brave, but in truth, I was scared all the time. If I heard a motorbike or car pulling up behind me, my body would break out in goose bumps and cold sweats. I also started having nightmares, nightmares about people following me. I didn't tell anyone. I wanted to protect my family, even if I didn't have anyone to protect me.

Life is like this in Guatemala. Once the wheels of violence are set in motion, they don't stop. They keep rolling forward. The engine may idle for a while, but the terrible machine will eventually keep plowing on, and it doesn't care who stands in its path; it rolls over you with impunity. Once you are in its sights, you can do little—maybe nothing—to save yourself . . . unless you see a door and you run through it.

———

Three years after the shooting, I was in my shop, fussing with the displays, rearranging the sequined dresses that would catch a woman's eye as she walked by, and organizing accessories—belts that would make you look skinnier, necklaces and earrings that would give your outfit that extra special touch—when an acquaintance stopped by to say hello and see how I was doing. The truth is, I told her, I was in a deep emotional funk. The sadness of Juan Alberto's death and what that meant for my children had never gone away, even if I was functioning better. Getting shot had left me even more unsettled and anxious, and I was still being harassed, even three years after the shooting. I was always waiting for the next terrible thing to happen, and a constant refrain ran through my mind: *What should I do? What should I do?* I was looking and looking, but I couldn't see a way forward, I couldn't see a way out. *"Díos Mío,"* I'd plead, "please open a door for me." And then, without prompting, without even telling my friend that I was contemplating leaving Guatemala, she said she would loan me the money if I wanted to make the trip to the United States.

There was no time to plan. I turned off the lights in the store, rolled down and locked the metal gate, and ran home. "Ma," I said, "I'm going." I didn't need to explain where; in Central America, the rest of that sentence writes itself. My decision was really that fast. I grabbed my youngest son, Fernando, stuffed a bag with essentials, and left. I couldn't even wait for Yordy, who was twelve, or my girls, who were eight and six, to come home from school, so I didn't say goodbye to them. The door of opportunity opened, and I ran through it because I knew with certainty, it was now or never. Yordy says that when he got home from school, he just knew—not because I'd ever talked about wanting to go to the United States, but because of the overwhelming look of sadness on my mother's face, which she was incapable of hiding from him.

For someone who has never lived under the crushing fear of constant threats of violence, my decision probably seems impossible to understand at best, and horribly selfish at worst. Most people won't give voice to their questions, but when I tell my story, I can see in the way their eyes change that they want so much to ask me, "How could you leave three of your kids behind? Why did you choose the child you took with you? Was it really impossible for you to wait a few hours to say goodbye? Who explained your choice to the children, and how?"

I see all of these questions flash across their faces, punctuated not just with question marks, but with exclamation points that underscore their judgment of me. They think, maybe, that I am selfish, that I don't care about all of my children. How do I explain to them that the most agonizing decisions I have made as a mother have all had to be made in a split second? In Central America's small towns, you can't give news time to travel. Every moment that you hesitate is an opportunity for your plan to reach one more set of ears. It gives someone time to stop you, to make your escape impossible. It could even give them enough time to grab a gun and stuff it in their waistband, eager for the opportunity to kill you.

Another question people want to ask but don't: "What about *your* mother? How could you saddle her with so much responsibility? An older woman who has worked so hard her whole life shouldn't have to raise her three grandchildren!" The notion of extended family—what it is and what our responsibilities are to one another—is hard for Americans to understand. In the United States, children grow up and leave home. They move far away, they leave their parents behind, and they start a family somewhere else—maybe even across the country. They see each other on occasion, maybe once a year, or twice, if they're lucky. In Guatemala, we grow up, we remain at home (or at least in the same town), we have children, and there *is* no "extended family."

We are simply family, and the roles and responsibilities of who cares for whom are not as rigid as they are in the States. We are all responsible to and for one another.

Was I sad to leave my mother, and did I worry about her? Of course! I was as sad to leave her as I was to leave my children. One of my greatest desires in life is to be by my mother's side always and to ease her worries and her burdens. Among the many things that people don't understand about migration is this: No one *wants* to leave the people they love. Most people don't want to leave the land where they were born, or the soil where their umbilical cord was buried. If they believed that staying would ensure survival, they would never set off on such a treacherous journey. They would never walk through that door, fighting the impulse to look back with the deepest longing a person is capable of feeling. But since they know they are at risk, they put one foot in front of the other and try not to look back, trying to hold themselves together, even as they feel that they're being ripped into two jagged-edge pieces that will never fit neatly together ever again.

————

When that door closes behind you, those you love are on the other side of it. They claw at the door, eventually becoming worn out from the effort and emotion, crumpled and crying, peering under the threshold and looking for your shadow. They may accept that you've left. They may even understand it. But to be left, the door slammed in your face, is something one never forgets. And you, the one doing the leaving, won't forget it either. Guilt and fear grip your insides, and while you know it was the only choice, you're still never quite sure it was the right one. You may not know until years later. The not-knowing gnaws at you constantly.

Years later, around a dinner table in New York, Yordy will tell friends how angry he was when I left, so infuriated and helplessly bereft that he went to an uncle's refrigerator and grabbed a beer, contemplating the idea of guzzling the whole thing in one desperate gulp. Instead, he hurled the bottle across the room, the glass smashing into a thousand little pieces, not unlike the pieces of his broken heart.

3

Hunger

I grew up hungry, always hungry.

Now, when I look at the only photo that I have of myself from my childhood, my adult eyes meet the insolent gaze of six-year-old Rosy and I remember her clearly. My heart aches for her. She has bangs that have been left uneven by a home haircut gone wrong. She's wearing an ill-fitting dress, and she stands sullenly in a spot where a large rock hides her feet so the viewer will never know what she and the photographer know, what they agree to maintain as a shared secret: Rosy owns no shoes. The only pair she had, some flimsy sandals, are broken and can't be repaired, and her mother has no money for new ones. She doesn't even have money for food.

Six-year-old Rosy's cheeks are full—or that's how they appear, anyway, so convincing in their ruddy roundness that Yordy, nearly thirty years later, exclaims, "Ma! Look how chubby you were!" when he sees the blurry photo for the first time.

"That's not chubbiness," I correct him. "That's the bloat of hunger." As soon as I say it, his expression deflates. His face is consumed by sadness, and I regret my words immediately.

It's not that Yordy doesn't know what it means to be hungry, but I spent the interminably long days of my earliest years either cradling my belly or trying to ignore its insistent growls. My father died when I was three, and that was when a deep, hard hunger set in. Before his death, my mother grew flowers next to our home, which was surrounded by several acres of coffee plants, and we grew food there, too, enough to keep us fed even when times were especially rough. When my father died of tongue cancer, everything, it seemed, started to change. Suddenly, we were poorer than poor. We were "look in the cabinet for a tortilla and not find one" poor. The speed with which you can move from "ordinary" poverty to extreme poverty is dizzying and terrifying, and I feel so deeply for my mother's struggles, how much she tried to care for us, how hard she worked, knowing it still wasn't enough, and how impossible many of her choices must have felt to her.

One of my father's brothers came to live with us, intending to keep my mother company because our house was far from town, in an isolated wooded area, and he wanted to help her. The idea, I think, was that he would support us financially, that he'd keep up my father's coffee parcel, that he'd protect us. But it was a troubled period in Guatemala: there was civil war; there were guerrillas; death was everywhere. My father, before he died, wanted nothing to do with any of it. While other people fled, he insisted that we weren't going to move because, why should we? He wasn't involved in politics or any illicit activity, and so he believed he had no reason to flee. "If death comes, let it come," he said. "We're not going to move because of fear." When he went out to work the coffee plots, he'd take a white flag with him and tie it to a tree or to himself so that if people saw him, whether on the ground or via aerial surveillance, they'd know he was just working—that he wasn't interested in any of the politics. But death, of course, kept coming.

At the time, my mother had a little business selling beans, which she traveled to Mexico to source. The trip typically took two or three days: one day to travel to Mexico and buy the beans; one day to stay in a house near the border, where she would clean the beans and package them so she could return to Guatemala with the beans undetected, in order to avoid having her tiny profit eaten into by an import tax; and one day to travel back home. Sometimes, she would go back and forth across the border with my older sister, Elvira, who was basically born working—like my mother, she hasn't gone to school a day in her life.

The rest of us would stay behind, some with grandparents and others with paternal aunts and uncles. We were scattered like corn seeds across the corners of a field. With the exception of the uncle who lived with us, they all hated my mother. They mocked her indigenous background and the fact that she spoke the Mayan language Mam. Their cruelty knew no bounds. They would pull her hair and push her around. She had no family of her own to help her, and they knew that, so they humiliated her in a thousand ways.

My aunts and uncles also wanted my father's land, and they were scheming for a way to reclaim it from my mother. These aunts and uncles would fill our minds with poisonous thoughts about our mother. "You *know* she's responsible for your father's death," one aunt would say with a sneer. "If she had let him sell the house, they would have had enough money to pay for his cancer treatment. She didn't want him to get better. If it weren't for her, he'd be alive today."

They didn't believe my mother when she explained that the doctors in the capital, where she had taken him for treatment, said he wasn't going to get better, that there was no cure. The doctors had performed two operations and had removed part of his tongue. They could do no more. "There is no hope," they told my mother. "He should stop traveling back and forth. Take him home and wait for death to come." Her in-laws abused her incessantly for following the doctors' advice.

"She's a *puta*," a loose woman, another would say with such disgust that she always sounded like she wanted to spit. "She leaves you with us because she doesn't care about you enough to keep you with her," they'd add, oblivious to the hurt they caused us. That hurt wasn't just emotional, either. The aunts would often say these horrible things as they used a rough scrub brush to bathe us. With each rasp of the brush, it felt as if they were scrubbing their harmful opinions deep into our tender flesh.

When you are young, your mind is so susceptible to anything adults tell you. This is especially true when they say something over and over again. Repetition is a powerful weapon. It has the effect of blurring or erasing whatever memories and truths you've stored, replacing one narrative, the one you know to be true, with another one, which might be incomplete or entirely false. And it's easy for the child's imagination to make leaps of logic because children lack life experience. Maybe our mother *didn't* care enough, some of my siblings thought, since she was hardly ever around. Maybe she *was* a *puta* since she was pregnant again. It didn't occur to them that she was working her fingers to the bone just to be able to earn our daily bread.

The chorus of these aunts' and uncles' voices has had a terrible, lasting impact on our family. The insults and lies were a long-acting venom, making it difficult for some of my siblings to ever really trust our mother fully. They also, in many cases, didn't even trust themselves, making decisions that would have ruinous effects on their own lives. And it made some of them very hard, tough in places where they might otherwise have been tender.

———

Once, after one of her bean-buying trips, my mother came home and knew something was amiss: strange men she didn't know were standing on the patio of the house, their chests puffed out and their booted feet firmly planted, as if they owned the place. She could tell that they were armed and that they meant business. There was blood. My brother's mouth had been covered so he wouldn't make noise while they tortured my uncle, the one who had moved in to protect us. I was young, but you don't forget these images: drops of blood were everywhere. Even the leaves of the plants in the yard were speckled red.

Days later, a body was found at the town's entrance. The rumor was that it was my uncle's corpse. We would never know what provoked this cruel fate, nor who was responsible for his death. My mother, terrified, packed us up and we left. "Even if we have to move from house to house," she said—and we did; we moved to eleven or twelve places before we finally found our own home—"we can't live here anymore." She shut the door behind us, and we began an itinerant life, moving for brief periods of time into the homes of people who were only slightly better off than we were, and who would take us in temporarily—but not without exacting their own price.

———

The absence of food makes thoughts of it loom large in your every waking moment, coloring the way you see people and how you feel about them. Though we moved often and much of our lives was a blur, I still can't forget, even decades later, the sharp memories, painful and clear, of how others used food to exclude or shame us. When we went to live with a woman in the border town of Camojá, she would say to my mother, "You can cook after I cook." But when she finished cooking, she'd tamp out the fire meticulously, cruelly. There was nothing left but little bits of burnt wood, ash really. My mother would have to go find her own wood, and we'd have to go help her look for sticks on the banks of the river so that she could cook for us.

Even on the morning my mother gave birth to our youngest sister, Brenda, whom she would give up for adoption because she knew she could not feed her, the woman with whom my mother was living and for whom she was working told her, "You may have pain, but you're not in labor yet. Make my tortillas. I have to have something to eat while you have the baby." My mother took the ball of masa, the mixture used to pat tortillas into thin discs, and channeled the pain of contractions into each kneading motion, into each slap of the masa as it took shape in her hands. I wonder now whether those tortillas tasted bitter, flavored with my mother's resignation and rage.

When you are hungry, you do absurd things, things you wouldn't do were your stomach not goading you on like some hungry devil—things like killing a little puny chicken that wasn't even yours. That's what my sister Elvira did once when my mother had gone to Mexico to buy her beans to resell in Guatemala. Too many days had passed without our having anything to eat, and when Elvira saw the chicken, she devised a plan for us to chase it into the house and trap it. To say it was a chicken is actually generous—it was so small! But she killed it. She wrung its neck—*snap!*—and she sliced its throat with a sharp kitchen knife, draining the blood, its metallic smell filling the air in the stifling shack. She plucked the feathers and cooked the bird. Afterward, she dug a little hole in the yard and buried the feathers and carcass, hoping no one would find out what she had done. What she didn't know is that the other chickens would scratch the hole open again and our act would be discovered. When she tells the story now, she laughs at first. But then she cries, tears slipping silently down her cheeks as her chest heaves. It's hard for us to think about what we did out of sheer necessity, and even harder to talk about it.

Initially, I was the only one who lived with my mother as she moved from job to job and house to house. My brothers and sisters had been convinced of my mother's unfitness to care for them by the lies of my aunts and uncles, and it would take time, and talking, and scheming ruses before she would get some of them back, reclaiming them from the bitter grip of our father's siblings.

One of the places we moved to was Guatemala City, the country's capital, so different from my hometown. Going from a rural small town to a busy city where cars and motos speed down wide, paved streets and some people wear suits and polished shoes and carry briefcases—there were many changes to absorb, so much to see and try to understand in the bustling scene around me. But I was enchanted, and I remember this as one of the happiest, most secure periods of my childhood.

It was also, however, one of the shortest. In our three months there, we lived with a kind and generous family. I remember that there was a boy who would leave 10 cents or a piece of candy under my pillow when I went to school. In this home, we always had food. I could have stayed there forever, but my mother was restless, tormented by the fact that she didn't have all of her children in her care and that we lived so far away she couldn't even see them.

She had had a dream in which she was in a room in front of a judge. When she entered the room, my father was there. "What are you doing here?" he asked her.

"Nothing," she replied. "I'm working."

"You have no business here," he warned her. "Do you want me to take my *chompipitos* [my little turkeys], or are you going to take care of them?"

She awoke from the dream in distress. What were the little turkeys? She decided that the only thing they could represent were her children. She interpreted the dream to mean that our father—our dead father—was angry at her for not having all of their children in her care. Our brief, happy chapter in the capital ended, and we returned to my hometown, and to hunger.

———

Unfortunately, food isn't like money: you can't store it in your body like you store money in a bank. It fills and fuels you only for so long, depreciating quickly and never earning interest. This is a lesson I learned too early in my life, and one I hoped my children would never have to learn. But for three generations, if not more, our family has been dealt the same set of cards over and over again: the too-early deaths of the people who anchored our family; poverty so extreme that even the hardest of work can't overcome it; and, yes, persistent, gnawing hunger.

Years earlier, when my mother was just about the same age that I am in that old photo, she lost her own mother. My grandfather worked the land and harvested the goods he sold, and he often spent long days away from home. One day, when my mother was seven, my grandfather asked my grandmother to join him on one of those trips; my mother would stay at home. My grandmother seemed to sense that the trip would be cursed, but a woman in those days didn't question her husband's judgment or his decisions.

Instead, she prepared quietly for the trip and did two things that haunt my mother to this day. First, she braided my mother's hair and told her to keep it nice and neat. "If I return," she whispered, "I will take it down and braid it again for you. But if I don't return, leave your hair in the braid to keep it tidy." Second, she called my mother aside, beyond the view of my grandfather, and pressed a key into her small hand. "This is for the box where I keep our money," she said in a quiet voice. "Do not lose it. And if I don't return, do not ever give this key to your father. If you do, he will drink away the money and you will have nothing."

My grandfather prepared their horse as a storm brewed on the horizon. My grandmother didn't speak her worries aloud, but they must have been visible. My grandfather chided my grandmother gently and told her that she could stay behind if she wished; if the gathering storm frightened her, she should remain at home. "No, no," she said obediently, "I will go with you." My mother watched them ride away, disappearing into the horizon. She went inside and locked the door, trembling as she thought about her mother's words and actions.

————

A few days later, my grandfather returned home. My grandmother was not with him. She was swept down a river by a current that was so powerful it ripped a leg from her body. What remained of her body was tangled in a tree.

She was gone.

Dead.

My mother's braid.

The key.

My grandfather, a typical man of his generation, showed no emotion and was unable to comfort my mother, much less care for her. Life was hard, with dangers and disappointments and death. What could you do? You couldn't bring the dead back to life, so you just kept living. Mourning was a luxury, a waste of valuable time. My grandfather kept on with his work as a harvester. My mother, meanwhile, was left home alone for increasingly long periods of time, and she spent her early years in constant terror.

Afraid because she was left to fend for herself and all of her needs, she decided she would be safer in the top of a tree, so she climbed up, hiking her skirt up as she scaled the trunk. During the day, she would sit in the treetop to monitor the comings and goings below, without anyone knowing she was there, alone. At night, once the sun had set, she shimmied back down the trunk and crawled under her bed. She tied her dog to the bedpost and taught him to bark if there was danger or to scare people away if they got too close. She never had enough love, and she never had enough food.

She met my father when she was fourteen, and things weren't much better. He used food as a punishment or as a reward. He'd taunt her, giving her a little cup with a scrap of food. "Who's that for? Who eats so little food?" she'd ask. "Oh, that's for you," he'd reply.

When her father died, what little support she had was gone completely.

Now, when I think about the common threads of our family's intergenerational stories, I am overcome with a deep, indescribable sadness.

———

Fernando, my youngest child, learned the hardest lessons about hunger on our first trip to the United States in 2014. When you pay a coyote or fixer, the sum is supposed to be all-inclusive. For between $3,000 and $5,000 per person, you'll have a guide, transportation, shelter, and food. That's the dream they sell you, anyway, like a vacation package in a glossy brochure.

But the reality is different. Coyotes and middlemen, such as drivers, are always trying to trim expenses so their own earnings are greater, and food is often the first line item that's eliminated from their budget. They will keep you going with the promise of food to come—"Oh, we'll eat later today, when we get to the hotel"—but an entire day might pass without food, and then another. On the rare occasions that they buy something to eat, it is likely to be old or almost inedible, like tough fried chicken you can barely chew, and it's often the case that there won't be enough to go around. Women and children are fed first, men last. I feel so sorry for the men, who are given even less food than we are.

Even if you manage to save up a little money and hide it somewhere on your body, you have limited opportunities to peel away from the group and duck into a store or shop to buy a snack or something to drink. And then, of course, once you're outside cities, being trucked through the vast desert spaces that stretch across so much of Mexico, you'll be hard-pressed to find a place to buy anything at all.

The trip can take four to six days, which doesn't sound like a long time, but it's long enough for a nursing mother's milk to dry up. Mine did, on the first trip, when Fernando was still breast-feeding. I watched other women grasp one of their breasts and move it toward their child's mouth, massaging the breast, trying to coax the last drops of milk out of it. They would be as disappointed and as desperate as their babies when it yielded no more, and then they tried the other breast, urging it to provide just one more feeding.

The trip is long enough to fantasize about every delicious morsel that has ever passed your lips, and to spend hours contemplating your favorite foods. Though it was torture to do so, I liked to think about creamy rice tamales speckled with generous chunks of turkey, a dish my mother makes for special occasions. I could taste the glutinous, silky mouthfeel of the rice, the sweet, slick grease of the turkey, the earthy taste of the pumpkin seeds. With so much time on your hands, you contemplate in excruciating detail how your favorite dish is made, how the banana leaves are sliced directly from their tree or purchased in the market before being heaped with the masa, which is stippled with the succulent dark meat that is taken from a turkey that you raised and killed yourself. It has been stewed in a sauce that can take hours to make and is luxurious because it has so many ingredients, much like a Mexican mole: the pumpkin seeds, sesame seeds, red peppers, onions, garlic, tomatoes, and achiote, which gives the sauce its red color, all simmering into an enchanting brew that tastes like Guatemala itself. You imagine your mother's fingers, now curled a bit with arthritis and age, wrapping the tamales, one by one, into bundles that are like gifts. She ties each one off with a long strip of the banana leaf since she has no string, and she gently lowers the tamales into the depths of a large pot of boiling water in her outdoor kitchen. They will bubble away there for hours before being served, the bundles opened, releasing richly fragranced curls of steam.

When you have imagined your way through the entire recipe, replaying every moment you sat and watched your mother make tamales, and there's nothing left to imagine, you remember what it was like to eat the tamales alongside people you loved, despite everyone's defects and complications. Whatever conflicts existed between you were set aside so you could enjoy the meal.

You draw forth the timbre of your brother's satisfied and grateful "*Mmmm*," and you cherish the image of your mother's smile spreading across her wrinkling face. For just that moment, for just that meal, everything is right with you and your family and the world, making a memory you can hang onto forever.

The trip is long enough for your stomach to struggle to accept food and water when you finally have access to them again. It's also long enough to die, if the conditions are right.

It's long enough, too, for you to make choices that, when you think about them later, fill you with disgust, like eating mangoes full of worms or drinking dirty water from a creek where cattle stand to cool off. You grip the mango with both hands, its juice running between your fingers and down your chin, and you're so ravenous, you don't even avoid the worms; you just sink your teeth right into them and keep chewing.

It's long enough for you to start lying to your children, just like the guides lie to you. There were moments when Fernando would say, "I'm hungry, I'm tired, I'm thirsty." I'd say, "Oh, we'll eat soon. We'll have something to drink soon." It was a lie. I had no idea when we'd eat or drink again. But you have to keep up the lie to keep up the hope. Fernando, even as young as he was, understood that he had to be strong. He learned, at such a young age, how to hang on.

But those tastes . . . they never leave your mouth. Memories of hunger and shame—and the shame of hunger—stay with you forever.

4

The Migrant Highway

My brother-in-law calls the two-lane road between San Antonio Huista, my hometown, and Gracias a Dios, the last town before you cross from northwestern Guatemala into Mexico, "the Migrant Highway." It's a good description, and one that has been accurate for generations, even centuries; archaeologists have found artifacts from all over Mesoamerica that were deposited along this road long before it was paved. Perhaps, rather than the plastic water bottles and gallon jugs we leave behind now, ceramic jugs were left behind by our indigenous ancestors, discarded either because they became too heavy or because they broke and were no longer useful.

It seems that every decade or so, a new crisis erupts, prompting larger flows of migrants from Central America into Mexico and then onward to the United States. In my own lifetime, it was Guatemala's thirty-six-year civil war that dragged on and on between 1960 and 1996. I was born during the war years, and as I grew into girlhood, nearing adolescence, the war was still raging. Imagine being born and raised in a climate of such persistent fear and danger. Imagine growing up without knowing peace.

It is hard to explain to outsiders how profoundly this war touched every area of life in Guatemala, and if you have not lived through a war, it can be difficult—maybe impossible—to wrap your mind around the statistics of our war and what it wrought, much less the psychological, social, and economic damage it caused. Land grabs and territorial disputes resulted in the forced displacement of thousands of people, especially rural, indigenous people who had little to their names to begin with, and even less as a result of the war.

But in a way, they were the lucky ones. They survived. The civil war left more than two hundred thousand people dead—Guatemala's total population today is just shy of seventeen million, so this means roughly 1 percent of the entire country was massacred. Thousands upon thousands of women were rendered widows by the war, and, of course, untold numbers of children became orphans who were left to fend for themselves. It is a wonder that anyone in Guatemala can wake up in the morning and function at all, wounded as we all are.

For those of us who are from there and grew up in this environment, it is neither difficult to understand the causes of the war nor to comprehend how it raged on for such an interminable period of time. It comes down to what causes all war and conflict, really: a fight instigated by those people who have the most resources and want to acquire still more, which provokes those of us with the least resources to defend ourselves and to try to hold on to what we can in order to survive. The government, of course, is nowhere to be found because it's benefiting from the battle. Corrupt politicians and their big business cronies gorge themselves on the spoils of war while the rest of us starve and struggle to wring out an existence.

It's worth noting that it's not just poverty, land distribution, and lack of government intervention that have caused so many people to flee Guatemala. It's what stepped into the void where the government and international community should have been, taking their place and taking matters into their own hands. I'm referring, of course, to the drug cartels, which have provided some people with a modicum of financial stability, physical protection, and a bit of a safety net in exchange for their collaboration and compliance with the drug traffickers' strict and brutal codes of business.

Those who don't comply, those who wish to retain their dignity and their moral values, even if it means living in grinding poverty, are subject to great dangers. There is virtually nothing or no one to shield them from these dangers. They have only themselves, and when that's no longer viable, they have to look for a way out. You don't have to use drugs, or sell them, or even know anything about them to be affected by them in Guatemala and neighboring countries. The drug trade permeates every layer of our societies, leaving nothing and no one untouched.

———

It's not just the war and its effects that have sent people north along the Migrant Highway in search of safety and a more stable life. Other problems in Guatemala and neighboring countries have sent Central Americans north, too. Recurrent agricultural crises in recent years—coffee blights and other conditions caused by the effects of rapidly accelerating climate change—have resulted in waves of coffee harvesters moving in order to find work. And then, of course, there is the mass migration that has been in the news so much lately, referred to by the US media as "the migrant caravan," which people join because they fear for their lives and want to escape violence, extortion, and instability.

Each spike in mass migration seems to have an activating effect, like rain falling on the desert, but more sinister. Instead of beautiful blossoms sprouting from cacti, painting the landscape with unexpected color, the arid soil blooms red with bloodstains. Not long ago, the Migrant Highway was a road of death. Cartels battled one another for control of this corridor, which was a key thoroughfare for moving migrants, drugs, and money. Some people still refer to the area as "the great drug warehouse" of the Americas. Today, if you drive along the highway, you'll notice seemingly legal businesses, such as cattle farms, that stretch out in vast parcels. Locals whisper about cartel bosses using these farms to launder money as the beef cattle whip their tails lazily back and forth, batting flies away, while slurping water from weather-beaten wooden troughs.

For those of us who have lived on or near the Migrant Highway—or those of us who have traveled it—we can't blot out the memory of the blood that has been spilled along this road. It seems so pastoral and calm today, but the Migrant Highway has seen some of the most brutal moments of our local history. The worst one happened on November 30, 2008, and it's seared in the memory of everyone in our country who was alive at the time.

On that date, a much-anticipated horse race was held in the town of Agua Zarca, located on the highway about halfway between my hometown of San Antonio Huista and the Guatemala-Mexico border town of Gracias a Dios, where my boys and I would cross the border on our 2018 journey to the United States. That day, the village of Agua Zarca was electric with anticipation; the horse race was a big event that drew attendees from near and far. Races like these offer a break from the hard labor of daily life: planting or harvesting coffee or working in the cornfields, called *milpas*, which are squeezed into every available patch of viable soil; gathering firewood and bundling it in cloth before heaving it onto one's back and attaching a belt around the head so the weight of the wood is distributed across the body; washing clothes in the river; making tortillas by hand; and trying to keep kids safe, clean, and fed.

But the excitement about the Agua Zarca race was short-lived, shattered when rival gangs—the Mexican Zetas and Guatemalan Huistas—became embroiled in an hours-long shoot-out, which allegedly began after someone lost a million-dollar bet (though other reports blamed a territorial dispute).

Motorcycles, cars, bodies, and bullet casings—so many that police would run out of crime scene evidence bullet cards—littered the highway. Blood streaked the seats of cars and door handles. Keys remained in ignitions, and the lights of some cars were still on as drivers and passengers bled out on the roadside. Houses all along the highway became casualties, too, as did some of their occupants, including the owner of a local coffee farm and his son—both killed. Police counted more than 150 bullet holes in just one farm truck, which was found across the border the next day. Even the Chevy that was going to be awarded to the winner of the horse race was discovered amidst the wreckage. In the weeks and months that followed, updates about the Agua Zarca massacre dominated local and national news.

Reports vary, but nearly twenty people died in the gun battle, including innocent bystanders—mainly indigenous residents of Agua Zarca who got caught in the unrelenting crossfire of bullets shot from AK-47s and 9 mm rifles. Survivors took lifeless bodies into their homes, holding vigil as they waited for the authorities to come and claim them. The police wouldn't arrive until the next day, however. Marlene Blanco Lapola, director of Guatemala's Civil Police Force at the time, said that sending in officers and agents right away was "too risky." "It's the territory of criminal gangs," she said. The statement was a shocking, open acknowledgment that even the police and other public safety authorities were subservient to the cartels. For those of us who lived nearby, as my family and I did, Blanco's remarks were terrifying. It was utterly clear that no one was going to save or protect us.

The Agua Zarca massacre of 2008 wasn't the first such killing in our region, and it wouldn't be the last, but something about it—its extreme brazenness, the sheer number of bullets, its duration, or the fact that even the federal police were afraid to intervene and secure the scene immediately—seemed to strike fear in the heart of Álvaro Colom, our president at the time. In a press conference held a few days after the *matazón* (mass killing), President Colom admitted that narco gangs had taken over huge swaths of Guatemala, and, he added, "It will take a lot of time to take these [lands] back." He appeared to be at a loss when it came to articulating a plan for reclaiming Guatemalan territory from the narcos. His failure to do so terrified us all. When even your president feels incapable of protecting you, you know you are in severe danger.

The incident provoked a presidential response on the other side of our border, too. Felipe Calderón, who was president of Mexico at the time, sent a group of cabinet officials to tour the nearly four hundred miles of the Guatemala-Mexico border, proclaiming that he would devote a significant amount of money and military power to seal his country's southern border and to strengthen the eight official border crossing checkpoints.

More than a decade later, though, the Migrant Highway, while less violent and bloody (for the moment, anyway), is still remarkable for its porousness and its lack of police presence. In Gracias a Dios, there's a customs kiosk and a Mexican immigration guardhouse. Neither seems to be well-staffed, and personnel on duty tend to wave through every vehicle without so much as an inspection.

That's what happened when our group crossed in 2018; we went through without any difficulties. They're not even looking for the bribes that are called "little bites," or *mordidas*. They don't need to squeeze migrants for a few pennies or bills because they are allegedly paid larger—much larger—sums of money by human traffickers. And this, of course, is just at one of the legal checkpoints. There are God knows how many informal crossings, none of which are manned by authorities.

At certain spots along the Migrant Highway, you can look up into the mountains and see dirt or gravel roads threading across the hills; at one point, you can even see the border demarcated. Coyotes and border crossers who want to avoid any detection at all often try their luck on these side roads rather than cross at an official checkpoint. Everyone who lives in the towns along this route—even stubborn old-timers who would never consider leaving their homes, no matter what—knows at least one person who could organize a trip like this for you. In our town, we can point out several people who can plan your trip—for the right price, of course.

The absence of police and the laissez-faire management of other officials, such as Mexico's immigration officers, are precisely why this zone remains such a heavily trafficked section of so many Central Americans' journeys northward. The area has been described as a "black hole." That's one way of thinking about it. But borders and the roads between them are always complicated spaces, landscapes where dark shadows hide from view all manner of illicit activity. Sometimes, though, that activity is happening in plain sight. You may not notice it if you're not one of them, but Guatemalans, Hondurans, and Salvadorans who are fleeing violence and headed to the United States are passengers in private cars, microbuses, and chicken buses. If you're headed north on the Migrant Highway, open your eyes: we are all around you.

It's easy to see us if you know what to look for. The men wear ball caps and long-sleeved shirts or sweaters that are incongruent with the warm weather. They have overstuffed backpacks that are straining at the seams. The ones who have never traveled the Migrant Highway, who don't know anyone who has, or who are just so stubborn that they neglect a more experienced person's advice will be pulling a suitcase behind them. Somewhere along the way, and sooner rather than later, probably, it will get left behind.

There are other clues that give us away. At this point in the journey—it's still early—most of the women have a certain look in their eyes that sets them apart from the locals who live in the border towns like Gracias a Dios. For the migrants, fear and uncertainty are fresh, and they're trying to get their bearings, assessing their surroundings for potential dangers. This is before they are utterly exhausted, unable to muster the energy to hold their heads up at all. Eventually, their eyes will glaze over, they will pare their belongings down to the barest essentials, and they will dig ever deeper into their emotional reserves, willing themselves to just keep going. I know because I have been one of them.

The last stretch of the Guatemalan part of the Migrant Highway can tell you everything you need to know about Central American immigration. Large, new houses, built of expensive materials and decorated with flourishes that are less functional than ostentatious, stick out among more humble homes. They are built with drug money or with dollars sent home by Guatemalans who are living and working in the United States. The money, sent back as remittances, is an essential part of the national economy in our countries. It's critical at the family level, too. A significant number of families rely solely upon remittances for their total income. That's not because the family members in Guatemala don't want to work. It's because there are hardly any jobs, much less any that pay a living wage.

The money sent back to Guatemala via Western Union and similar services is used to buy food, to pay for children's education (in Guatemala, parents must pay for their child to attend even public school), and, among other things, to build or improve homes. The large, brightly colored homes along the Migrant Highway, some with fences, security cameras, and cupolas, stand in stark contrast to neighboring structures, some of which are made of wattle and daub and have no indoor plumbing or electricity. I've lived in the latter type of home. The other kind speaks to the wealth we believe waits for us and that will be the reward for our hard work if we can just make this journey successfully.

There are other immigration stories along the Migrant Highway that are waiting to be revealed. Stop by the convenience store on the right side of the road just before you reach Gracias a Dios proper, and it won't be long before the woman behind the counter asks you where you're from and where you're headed. While you sit on the step of her store and sip shrimp and chili–flavored Maruchan soup, she'll tell you her migration story. She lived in Virginia for years, working first for $5.50 an hour and, later, climbing up one more rung on the immigrant ladder, getting a "good job" at a chicken-processing plant. Why did she come back? At the good job, she explains, she had an accident and injured her ankle. She tried to file a claim for worker's compensation, but, she says, her employer wouldn't take responsibility for the accident and denied her any kind of financial compensation or time off. She kept working for as long as she could, but eventually, her ankle could no longer bear the weight of an eight-hour shift, plus overtime, spent entirely on her feet.

It's a common story. Although most states in the United States have laws that protect even undocumented immigrants from employers who seek to use their workers' immigration status to deny them benefits, immigrants who aren't aware of these laws and their rights simply don't seek relief or recourse—they don't know it exists. And even for those of us who know our rights in the United States, it can be hard for us to assert or claim them. I know because I felt that way, too. Grateful just to have a job, I wouldn't have dreamed of complaining or seeking relief for my damaged wrist when I worked at a factory in Chicago. I just bound it up in a splint and kept working. We are afraid, especially when we hear in the news the rhetoric of people who don't like immigrants and don't want us here. Like this woman, then, we may make the difficult decision to return to our home country.

"Without money in the US, you can't survive," the shopkeeper says, adding that she hopes her children will return to El Norte, "the north," even if she doesn't intend to make the journey again herself. Instead, she contents herself with the comings and goings of other migrants, packing black plastic bags with the food they pile on the counter to purchase before the next leg of their journey: Doritos and Lay's potato chips; spicy, tongue-blistering Takis rolled tortilla chips with boldly named flavors like "Fuego," "Nitro," and "Xplosion"; cellophane packets of salted peanuts; or Bimbo pastries stuffed with creams or jellies and drizzled with chocolate icing. Energy drinks are popular for washing it all down. She wishes the migrants well as they head up the narrowing highway. "Go with God," she says.

———

The last mile or so of road through Gracias a Dios is a gauntlet. On both sides of the road, which has shrunk to an oversize single lane that miraculously manages to accommodate two-way traffic, vendors call out excitedly or surreptitiously, depending on what they're hawking, all of them vying for the attention—and money—of passersby. If you're hungry, there are ears of locally grown corn and fresh tortillas cooking on grills, as well as a string of taco stands, each claiming to be the best in town. There are storefronts where you can grab a pair of cheap sunglasses made in China or individual packets of Tylenol or ibuprofen. Bored shopkeepers maintain watch over knotted-up piles of knock-off iPhone and Samsung Galaxy chargers that probably won't last the duration of the trip. Speaking of phones, you can top off your minutes and buy a new SIM card or a case to protect your screen from breaking. Men wearing bulging fanny packs lean into car windows, chanting "*Cambio, cambio* (Change, change)," and maybe, if they're daring, they wave a few bills in several different currencies. They may spread the bills out like a fan, to show that they're able to change whatever money you need: Honduran lempira into Guatemalan quetzales, Guatemalan quetzales into Mexican pesos, or Mexican pesos into US dollars.

It's a last-stop shop before you venture into a no-man's-land of sorts, one where your movements as a migrant will be much more controlled by your coyote or guide, and where you won't know when you'll have an opportunity to buy anything you need—if you have such an opportunity at all.

All sorts of informal businesses exist on the border. For instance, mounds of used clothing trucked all the way from the United States are piled on tarps on the left side of the road. They are so close to the border, it's as if someone couldn't off-load the trucks fast enough, shoveling used T-shirts and jeans and hoodies and leggings into enormous towering piles that could suffocate a child if they were to collapse. People pick through them eagerly, stuffing plastic sacks full of their finds. That's how a New York Yankees jersey ends up in rural Guatemala, worn by the teenaged son of a corn farmer, or how we learn the names of your national parks, your cities, your favorite pop culture performers and sports stars. It's how T-shirts emblazoned with unicorns and stitched with flip sequins became trends in Central America.

The used-clothing business is a booming industry. You'd be amazed, especially looking at this mess of clothes tossed on a roadside, to learn just how complex it is and how many people it involves. It's technically an illegal business, too, just as my mother's cross-border bean business was, so it relies upon a multinational chain of bribes, all paid out before shoppers in Gracias a Dios dive into the piles.

Other businesses on the border take advantage of what people have available to loan out for a price. Families rent out their toilets and sell you a handful of toilet paper if you need to use the bathroom, or a room if you're making the trip without a guide and you need a place to rest before you cross. If you *are* with a group, you may spend a night or two in a safe house, which guides pay for with the money you gave them for the trip. Women rent their bodies out to men who are looking for some temporary relief from the journey's stresses. They are available at all hours of the day and night, and they're not hard to find—their brightly stained lips, short, tight skirts, and breasts spilling out of their blouses being more effective than any business card or advertisement. I don't judge them: we all do what we have to do in order to survive and to take care of our families. One young man has turned his tuk-tuk, a popular form of transportation here, into a mobile fast-food shop; he sells tacos, soup, and steaming hot *champurrado*, a thick, sweet, corn-based drink, out of a clutch of coolers he's attached to the tuk-tuk with bungee cords. The tuk-tuk strains as he pushes the gas pedal to the floor, urging the overladen vehicle to climb the hill toward the border.

I've been to this town and other Guatemala-Mexico border towns dozens of times in my lifetime, both with my mother on her bean-buying trips and on my own two journeys out of Guatemala, bound for the United States. I've been holed up with my boys in a "safe" house here, an experience that allowed me to see beyond the town's busy, benign façade. The Migrant Highway is quiet now. The bloodstains at Agua Zarca are buried. But it's impossible to ride along the Migrant Highway and not think about the Agua Zarca massacre, even though there are no signs of it today—the roadside has new, happy attractions, like a family fun center with pools and water features, an arcade, and a restaurant, which only Mexicans can afford. At any moment, the façade could fall and everything could unravel. The border is a precarious place, where the only certainty is that people will continue to cross it, headed north, toward safety and, they hope, a better life for themselves and the people they love.

5

Trucks

I won't say that my first trip to the United States was easy—it definitely wasn't—but we made it, Fernando and I, and we settled into a home on the outskirts of Chicago. Each day, I left Fernando with an acquaintance before commuting close to the city's periphery to work at a factory where catalogs and other mass-mailed items were printed, bundled, and prepared for shipping. It was repetitive, tedious, exhausting work. The boss, who spoke only English and called me "Rose," was demanding; the machines broke frequently; and my back hurt constantly. So did my hands, which were perpetually swollen. One of my wrists was bound in a support splint that I rarely removed. At night, when I got home, I found that I could barely lift Fernando from the chair or floor, where he had fallen asleep, into the bed we shared; and I was alarmed by the fact that he was maturing more quickly than he should, often waking up and covering *me* with a blanket as I fell asleep in exhaustion.

For a Central American family, immigration of one or more of its members represents promise and hope. All of the challenges and realities of living abroad and existing on the lowest rung of the socioeconomic ladder are invisible to our families at home; they see only possibility. A rare, fleeting moment of happiness or peace that's posted to Facebook or Instagram can convey the wrong message, and it obscures the mind- and body-numbing realities of our day-to-day lives. Most months, I could barely make ends meet, and more times than not, I had to ask for credit, putting off one bill to pay another one. Between paying someone to take me to work, buying lunch, paying for someone to take care of Fernando, and paying for our rent, groceries, and laundry, it was a rare month when I had even a dollar left. But those were the parts of my life that were invisible to our family in San Antonio Huista. They also were the parts that were invisible to people who wanted to take advantage of my family because of my migration status.

Because I lived abroad, people were trying to extract money from my mother, my sister, our family. They presumed I had money and that, in turn, I was sending large remittances home to my family. But that wasn't the case. Even when my boss offered more hours, bumping me up to a schedule of twelve-hour days, six days a week, it was a lucky month when I could scrape together enough money to send a remittance to my family. When I did, my mother would spend it on my children's school tuition, their food, or my daughters' marimba lessons. She'd wrap whatever was left over—which wasn't much—into a cloth and tuck that deep into her bureau, keeping a careful accounting of the money. I told her to use it to help build and improve our home.

Still, anonymous callers had been ringing my mother's cell phone. One day, as she was working at her stall in the market, she received a call around noon. She didn't recognize the phone number, but she answered anyway. "*¿Bueno?*" she said, apprehensively. A man's voice responded to her greeting. "You'd better come up with 50,000 quetzales [about $6,500]," he demanded in a threatening voice. "If you don't have the money by 4 this afternoon, we'll kidnap and kill your grandson—the big one. We know what he looks like and where he goes to school," he continued. "We'll grab him, and that will be that."

My mother trembled as she listened to the caller's words. She is a fearful, anxious woman, but something inside told her that she had to stand up to him, that she had to speak the truth. She had never, not in her entire life, held 50,000 quetzales in her hands all at once. She could hardly come up with the 400 quetzales that she was obliged to pay the man who sold her the weekly bushel of tomatoes that she would turn around and sell—*if* they all sold—for a razor-thin margin of 100 quetzales, or about $13. More often than not, however, she wouldn't even be able to sell all of the tomatoes. By week's end, a pathetic pile of them would remain, their juice and seeds oozing out of the rotting flesh, attracting flies that would buzz around her stand until she removed the spoiled produce. The tomatoes were so past their prime she couldn't even salvage them for herself. There was just too much competition in the small municipal market, and not enough money in the town to guarantee that she could turn over her weekly inventory successfully. Besides, her market stand and *comedor* were tucked away on the second floor of the market, beyond the view—and the wallets—of shoppers who could buy what they needed from vendors on the first floor.

"I don't have 50,000 quetzales," she told the man. "I barely have 400 quetzales to pay for the tomatoes I buy to resell at the market." She stopped talking and drew a breath.

"We'll call you again in four hours, and you better have the money, or else," the man threatened.

"You can call in four hours, but I can't make that kind of money materialize out of nothing," she replied curtly, hanging up and dropping to her knees to pray like she had never prayed in her life, her voice quivering, but her words fervent.

When the news of this call reached me in Chicago, I was shaken to my core. I knew all too well how these kinds of calls end. Everyone in Central America does. The callers aren't making empty threats or promises they won't keep. They would have no problem grabbing Yordy as he came out of school, conscripting him into a gang against his will, or killing him and dumping his body by the roadside. Gangs want money or they want blood. Often, they want both. I told my mother that this caller's threats troubled me so much that Fernando and I would come home. She tried to discourage me from returning. She told me she had phoned Fernando's father, Nery, and told him about the threat, and that he had responded immediately, driving in from the nearby town of Cuatro Caminos, where he lives, to check on her and to strike some fear into the caller's heart. He stood on the patio of my mother's house and fired his gun into the air, warning shots that advised the caller to stand down and leave my family alone. For a brief time, the threats stopped.

I appreciated Nery's responsiveness, as did my mother and sister, who were sharing responsibility for caring for my children and were living in terror, but I felt sure that brandishing his gun would have only a temporary effect. Yordy was now a teenager, of the age when even if this caller didn't grab him and force him to do his bidding, another gang or criminal element could. Our country has many gangs, and they are considered to be among the most sophisticated and dangerous in Central America. Terrible superlatives, but accurate ones. I suppose the war years gave men the time and experience to perfect their threatening techniques. Because so many of our police and military forces are also complicit in the gangs' activities, we can't rely on the so-called public safety officials to protect us. I knew this after having experienced Juan Alberto's death and having survived the attempt on my own life. I knew it after Agua Zarca, when the police were quaking in their boots. Ninety-five percent of all crimes go unpunished in our country. The writing was on the wall: I needed to get Yordy out of Guatemala.

So, this is why Fernando and I left Chicago, why we made the reverse trip to Guatemala, where life is untenable for a teenage boy who has already been threatened. And it wasn't just any boy. Yordy was *my* boy. If he was harmed, how could I ever live with myself?

Families in Central America are accustomed to comings and goings, migrations and deportations, of family members, the family unit expanding and contracting in a constant state of flux. With each movement, the family members who remain in the home country adjust their responsibilities and absorb the anxieties of those of us who have left or returned. The dynamic is a complicated one, albeit one to which we are resigned.

When Fernando and I returned to Guatemala from Chicago, my children were happy that we were home, but I also noticed that something had changed. With my mother having moved from the role of the kids' grandmother to one of a more maternal figure during my absence, my return raised questions about whether both of us could exert authority over them, especially over my two daughters. I missed key milestones in their development and important moments in their lives; it was natural for them to be resentful about that or slightly distant as a result, even if they never said a word of complaint.

What made my return harder was knowing that I was going to be leaving Guatemala again, this time with both boys. It would take me a couple of years to be able to get everything in order to make this second journey to El Norte, but the thought of the trip was never far from my mind. I was taking Yordy because of his vulnerability and Fernando because he was so young. He still *needed* his mother. Once more, I would leave my daughters behind, and they would experience that pain anew. Maybe this time, I worried, it will be worse, though. To be left twice would be particularly challenging. Would it create irreparable harm in our relationship?

Leaving my daughters behind would be agonizing. I knew they were in safe and loving hands with my mother and my sister and all of our wonderful, supportive family members, but since I also knew how it felt to be a girl who is apart from her mother and wants nothing more than to be with her, my body was wracked with the physical manifestations of the stress. My head hurt, and so did my heart. My whole body felt heavy. My stomach and intestines felt as if they were twisted up tightly, and I didn't want to eat. What could I do to show Britny and Dulce how much I loved them? How could I explain that leaving would not negate that love?

But if we didn't leave, I could lose my son. It was not an improbable scenario. I told myself, *This is for a short time. The girls and I will be together again.*

So, we pack a small bag and then we're off, headed toward the Guatemala-Mexico border, winding our way along the Migrant Highway—Fernando for the second time. We pass the water park, and I wish with all my heart that my country were safe, that we could make a living here, that we could celebrate special moments and make beautiful memories at a fun, exciting place like this. I wish we did not have to live with so many recollections of bloodshed and hardship. I wish that the map of our country wasn't stippled with the coordinates of collective horror and pain that have accumulated over decades.

When we get to Gracias a Dios with the group of other Central Americans who are traveling with us, the trip organizer bows his head and calls us all to prayer. "It will be a difficult trip," he says solemnly, "and you should support one another. Go forth in God's hands."

———

In Gracias a Dios, the trip organizer gathers our group of several dozen in a safe house, where he tells us we'll wait until some trucks come to pick us up. The house is two stories tall, and we are all crowded into a single room on the second floor. There are people from Honduras, people from El Salvador, people from Guatemala. Women and men. Children. Babies. Seeing them all here hurts me so much—all of us fleeing our beautiful, broken countries because of violence.

Time is always your enemy on a trip like this. As we wait for the trucks, I have too much time to think, and I start to have second thoughts about my decision to leave again. Maybe we *should* stay. On the way here, the driver stopped for gas in the town of Cuatro Caminos, and I happened to run into a cousin. She asked me where I was going, and I told her I was on my way to Petén to see one of my sisters. When we said goodbye, she kept looking at me—maybe the sadness was written on my face—and said, "You're going to the United States again, aren't you?" I fought to hold back my tears. I bit my lip, shook my head, and told her no.

"Tell me the truth," she said sternly, looking straight into my eyes. She was with other people, so we moved off to the side so we could speak privately. I told her I *was* leaving, and she asked why. I didn't want to tell her all the details, but I said I couldn't stay in Guatemala anymore. She hugged me and started crying and wished us well. She said goodbye to Yordy, who was so beloved by everyone, and said goodbye to Fernando, too. We hugged again. The truck that was transporting us was ready to go, so we had to get on it.

Now, here we are in this safe house, a group portrait of miserable, terrified people. I know for certain it will get worse before it gets better. *Maybe we* should *stay*, I think to myself again, my heart and mind swinging wildly back and forth between the opposite decisions of staying versus going. I look at Yordy and remember the threats. We have to go. I know in my heart it has to be this way.

Looking around at those who are going to make the journey with us, it is evident that the trip will be hard, even in a best-case scenario. There are so many women with children. There are pregnant women, too. I already know that the children will cry and the mothers will panic, doing everything possible to try to keep them quiet: holding them closer, rocking them gently, and even forcing their hands over the children's mouths to muffle any sound. They will plead with their children, no matter what ages, to understand that they have to be silent. The cleverest among the mothers will turn this into a game, trying to make being quiet fun. The stress of doing all these things will sap their energy, which will make them more vulnerable to the trip's innumerable other stresses.

In our group, one man has a club foot. People with disabilities are incredibly vulnerable in Central America; they are discriminated against, made fun of, and pushed to the margins. They rarely receive any special support or services, and many are never allowed to go to school. Work opportunities are even more limited, and so they are often forced to live their lives as beggars, endangering themselves, for example, by holding out a cup and asking for money at busy intersections. It is not hard for me to understand why they fled, even when the odds of their making the journey successfully seem so slim. We haven't even made it out of Guatemala and the man with the club foot, who is traveling with his fourteen-year-old son, already looks exhausted. His presence will make the trip more challenging for us, too, as those of us who feel compassion and a sense of responsibility are obliged to keep an eye on him. For instance, we will need to help him in and out of the trucks.

This trip is different from my first one, when Fernando and I took different forms of transportation, including buses, out of Guatemala and into and across Mexico. We were accompanied by guides, who bought our tickets and rode along with us. It wasn't necessarily easier, and it had its own dangers, especially for women. Guides often tried to cop a feel while on the long bus rides, attempting to trap a woman in a window seat near the back of the bus while he took an aisle seat, so as to control her movements. At night, they created ruses to try to corner a woman in a hotel room with them. That happened to me on the first trip. A guide said, "Oh, we've run out of rooms for the women, so you'll have to share my bed with me—just for tonight." I grabbed my bag and my child and told him I'd rather sleep on the floor of the another woman's room than in a bed with him.

Initially, this trip was looking up compared with that one. This time, the trip's organizer, who also made the plans for my last trip, had decided he won't use guides; he'd had too many problems with them, too many complaints. This time, he had decided to hire drivers with big trucks. He could move more people that way and move them more quickly and more directly. More people meant more money, too. He'd maintain contact with the drivers throughout the trip, tracking our progress across Mexico and waiting to hear that we'd made it safely across the Mexico-US border and into Arizona, which is our destination.

The first truck arrives, and a group is hustled out of the safe house. A woman from the town of Chinacá, who has brought along her four-year-old son, struggles to lift her bulging suitcase. The trip organizer looks on and says flatly, "That's too big; you can't take it. There's no way you'll be able to carry it." She is flustered and annoyed, complaining that she has already left one suitcase behind; she can't possibly leave this one, too. She unzips the luggage and we all look on as she scrutinizes each item, contemplating what she is willing to part with. There are boots and tennis shoes and flip-flops, a pair of shoes for every season and occasion, it seems. I marvel that she has also packed high heels, as if there will be a fancy desert dance party somewhere along the way that calls for us to dress up and strap on a pair of stilettos. When she finishes sorting through everything, the bag is still oversize. The organizer just sighs as the woman huffs, "Okay. Fine. Let's go." One wonders what happens to the things that get left behind, the still serviceable but abandoned objects that are strewn along the chain of safe houses and hotels, along the roads and trails that mark the map of our journeys.

A second truck pulls up, and it is our turn to crowd into the vehicle. I scramble into the truck bed with Fernando and turn to see that Yordy is being assigned to a third truck, which will be filled with men only. I don't want to be separated from him, but there is no chance to protest the decision. Everyone is squished into the truck, the human equivalent of chicken or cattle you see crowded into crates or pens and loaded onto trucks to be shipped from the farm to the slaughterhouse.

It's impossible to exaggerate how terrifying it is to be human cargo. The trucks fly along the roads at outrageous speeds, as if the drivers can't wait to get rid of us and pick up their next load and, of course, their next payment. Pedal to the metal, they hit potholes at full tilt, the bumps rattling our teeth and our bones. It seems the drivers have forgotten we are back here, or they just don't care. The latter is more likely.

I am convinced that the constant bumps are what cause one pregnant woman to miscarry along the way. My heart breaks when I think about all the losses that have occurred along the Migrant Highway, each one a story that will be remembered

only by the person who suffered it. If these losses were identified by tombstones, the whole highway would be lined by an
unbroken chain of marble or humble concrete markers. "Here
lies a woman's virginity." "Rest in eternal peace, stillborn infant."
"RIP HOPE." The memorials of pain would be so poignant that
you'd have to look away.

A hundred or so miles northwest of Gracias a Dios, the truck
grinds to a halt in San Cristóbal, a large town right in the heart
of the Mexican state of Chiapas. One person after another climbs
out of the truck, and I'm finally able to stretch my legs and
breathe deep lungfuls of clear air. The drivers tell us that if we
want to eat, we'll need to buy something for ourselves, and they
gesture to a nearby store. Fernando and I meet up with Yordy,
who has climbed out of his truck looking pale and shaken. He
doesn't say a word; he just looks terrified. I rush to console him,
pulling him into an embrace. I tell him the first of many lies: that
the worst of the trip is behind us.

I have no idea the worst is yet to come.

The drivers don't tell us how long we have before we will
leave San Cristóbal, but I know it could be mere minutes or
seemingly endless hours. In case it's the former, I hurry the boys
across the street to do our shopping. We buy bottled water and
some snacks. It's just what we can carry and it won't last nearly
long enough, but what a relief it is to gulp the water greedily and
feel it cool our parched throats.

When we get back to the trucks, the drivers tell us to wait
behind some nearby houses, which are surrounded by San

Cristóbal's densely forested mountains. The geography of this Mexican state that borders Guatemala is favorable for human traffickers: the jungle is often enveloped by a thick, heavy fog; the mountains have a limited police presence; and five main routes are available that coyotes have mapped out and deemed most viable. One is by water, but the others are by land. Ours is one of the land routes, and our drivers know it better than they know the roads of their own hometowns. They have business relationships with all the people they have to pay off along the way, and they don't want to deviate from this path if they can avoid doing so. Any detour presents dangers they don't want to confront and, inevitably, expenses they don't want to absorb.

Three trucks, different from the ones that brought us here, pull around to the back of the houses, and a driver divides us into groups. Each group is given a nickname, a silly name, like Lizards or Pirates, and we're told to climb aboard, where we'll fold ourselves up again like origami humans, sitting that way for who knows how long. The nicknames rub me the wrong way, as if we are nothing but pieces in a childish game that our drivers play for their own private amusement. I feel a tremendous irritation that I can barely contain.

Then, something inside me snaps, and I hear myself say, defiantly, in a steely voice, "I'm not going in a truck." I tell Yordy to stand back and let everyone else get on. If I get on a truck, it's not going to be without both of my sons. Two of the trucks fill up, and the remainder of our group is boarding the third. The driver is impatient. "Are you getting on or not?" he asks in a voice that indicates he couldn't care less what my answer is. "There's nothing else coming for you," he adds. I'm trapped, and I know it. If we bail now, we're on our own, thousands of dollars wasted, with little money to sustain us until we reach the United States. And that's *if* we reach the United States. How will I navigate the way there on my own, with two children in tow? So, we get on the truck and I look to heaven. "God," I say, "you have always protected us." At least the three of us are together this time.

This truck, the third one, is less crowded, and we're slightly more comfortable. In the other two trucks, passengers are packed in like sardines—just as tight and just as stinky—their knees pulled close to their chests, as they sit on top of their bags. But even with the extra bit of space, Yordy is stressed. He can't move much at all and the heat is suffocating, made more oppressive by the smell of everyone's bodies, sweat mixed with dust and desperation. The desperation is mental, emotional, and physical, the mind, heart, and body all tensing themselves in self-defense in an exhausting effort to ward off needs. It's a specific, sour smell that clings to the body and settles in the nostrils, a smell you will never forget.

I don't notice my own discomfort because I'm so preoccupied by Yordy's distress. Within an hour, our legs are completely numb. A heavy plastic tarp covers the top of the truck, so it's as dark as a cave inside the truck bed; we can't see a thing. All we can feel is the truck gaining speed and careening around curves, our bodies tensing with each mountainous switchback. There's nothing to grab ahold of to steady ourselves, and so we fall into each other's bodies, developing a unique, forced intimacy that can be formed only in these kinds of situations.

We don't talk about it—we don't talk much at all, really—but we have all heard stories of migrants who have died on the journey—not just the ones who have died of thirst in the desert, but also the ones who have died because the vehicles carrying them soar off cliffs without guardrails, plummeting into deep, rocky canyons, or slide into mountain faces and overturn, throwing passengers out onto the roadway, snuffing out their hopes and dreams along with their lives.

In the back of the truck, your mind goes to terrifying places. Since you can't see, you don't know what's happening; you just imagine things. You replay images of terrible, tragic videos you've seen on Facebook or YouTube, which get passed around Central America faster than a funny meme. There's one, for example, in which families of twenty-three Guatemalan migrants killed along the journey (in Chiapas, no less, where we are right now) because of the driver's excess speed take their own pilgrimage to reclaim the bodies of their loved ones. What despair! As the truck carrying the dead bodies slows down and pulls over on the edge of the highway, the waiting family members, all dressed in black, race to jump onto the vehicle. They vault into the truck bed and climb atop the cardboard boxes containing the corpses, throwing their arms across the boxes as if love and tears and moans that come from the deepest part of their being could bring the dead back to life. You play back these videos, and then you insert your own loved ones into the frames: your mother or your sister becomes the keening woman clad in a black polyester skirt and button-down blouse who wails "*¡Ay, Dios Mio!*" You or, God forbid, your child is in one of the body-size cardboard boxes. How, you wonder, will they get the box back to your hometown? Who will take flowers to your funeral? How will they pay for your service? How will everyone go on?

In the truck, you think of these things and you pray. You ask God to be with you.

At one point, there is a roadblock. In the world of human trafficking, there are a hundred actors with bit parts. One of them is the *bandera*. The literal translation of this word is "flag," and the role of the *bandera* is to be a sort of pilot vehicle or advance scout, reporting back to truck drivers about any dangers or concerns that lie ahead. The *bandera* for our trio of trucks spots a checkpoint and warns drivers to pull off the road and wait things out.

When a driver is out of his own territory, has deviated from his intended route, or just runs into a bit of bad luck, he can never be sure whether officers will inspect his truck and happen upon his human cargo. If discovered, the driver could be arrested and his truck—his livelihood—impounded. Or he could just be shaken down for a major cut of his earnings. Neither scenario appeals to him because both represent losses of time and money.

Our drivers find a spot to pull over, and they step out of their cabs to bark out their warnings: "Shut up. Keep the kids quiet.

Don't stand up because they'll see you, and if they see you, that's it, we're all fucked. Don't talk. If you talk, they're going to hear you." There are so many rules. The only thing they don't tell us is that we can't breathe—even though we can barely do that.

We sit, cramped, in utter silence. We work together to keep the kids quiet, but one baby cries and cries and cries. His mother has to practically suffocate him so we won't draw unwanted attention to ourselves. Of course, this makes him scream more, and we're all desperate, unable to do anything to keep him quiet.

We wait in this way for an hour or two—it's hard to know how long because your sense of time elongates and contracts inexplicably, distorting minutes and hours like a funhouse mirror distorts your body when you're standing in front of it. Finally, someone breaks. We are all tired. One of the passengers decides he can't take it anymore; he has to move. And then everyone wants to move, everyone wants to see, everyone wants to talk. One by one, passengers take turns peeking outside the truck, and once it's deemed safe, we step out to stretch our legs. Someone tiptoes around to the truck's cabs, only to find that the drivers are asleep! They had all of us here, folded up, in pain and terror, while they snored peacefully in the driver's cabin!

Nobody dares to wake them. These men are hired for their quick temper, for their fearlessness. Instead, we all spread out and try to find a place where we can sit outside the truck and stretch our legs and rest until they decide it's time to move on. I walk around the perimeter of the area, assessing our options, but there is nowhere to sit. The terrain is rocky, mountainous. Even if you could find a comfortable spot, you don't want to get *too* comfortable—you could fall asleep and the drivers could leave you. Then what would you do, a woman, alone with two children in this landscape, far from civilization?

When the men wake up, they tell us we can't leave yet—the checkpoint is still in effect and until it's dismantled, we can't go forward. Though we're out of the truck and breathing fresh air, the desperation is increasingly acute and palpable. We don't have food. We're out of water. The smell of human waste permeates the air.

By 4 p.m., even the drivers are restless. They're hungry, too, so they head off in search of some food. Their standards are low, and when they return, they're lugging bags of tough chicken and bread. I had dental work done recently, so I can't eat what they have to offer us. A pregnant woman can't eat the chicken and bread, either. Her nausea is intense, and it's not helped by the fetid smell of our surroundings. Some of the other passengers make fun of her, relieved, perhaps, that someone is in greater pain and discomfort than they are—people can be like that. Maybe, too, they're making fun of her because you can tell she's a woman who comes from a family with resources; she has a nice suitcase and her husband is traveling with her. They call her "delicate" and laugh. The woman complains about how much her back aches. The cause could be the harsh ride, the typical discomforts of pregnancy, or dehydration, I think; regardless, I'm worried about her. This journey isn't easy for anyone, and it's especially hard for a woman who is carrying another life inside her. The drivers have brought nothing to drink, and they have no reason, nor apology, for this.

As I'm sitting on my rock, observing the scene, the children either play with pebbles or sit as listlessly as the adults, exhausted and staring into space. Once in a while, they ask for food or drink, their faces falling when their parents can produce nothing to share with them. Sometimes, they say they have to pee, and the parents look about, trying to identify a safe spot that hasn't already been soiled by a previous migrant. I notice that one of the trucks—the one in which the pregnant woman had been riding—has a ruptured gas tank. *There's no way I'm getting in that truck*, I say to myself. The men try to fix the tank, but without success. The men who are hired for these jobs aren't exactly the most intelligent people. One can't utter enough prayers that we will be safely delivered to our destination, given that we are in these men's rough, uncaring, incapable hands.

Suddenly, the drivers announce that the guards at the checkpoint have left their posts, so it's time to go, quickly, quickly. We load up, relieved to leave this wasteland, though we know we'll soon be facing discomfort again. Despite my thought that I wouldn't get in the truck with the ruptured gas tank, that's exactly where we end up. I'm terrified, but I say nothing to Yordy or Fernando. What if this truck explodes and we all go up in a ball of flames? That's not the way I want myself or my children to die. I don't want my family to have to make their way here to claim our charred remains. I try not to think about the tank and to turn my thoughts, instead, toward God. *Please, have mercy on us*, I pray. *Be with us. Please, Lord, do not abandon us.*

Hours later, deep into the night, the trucks stop. We can hear something happening, but it's impossible to discern what's going on. There's the sound of feet scrambling across dirt and gravel, and many voices shouting, but we can't make out any words. A gunshot rings out into the air. The darkness is so complete that those of us in the truck bed can't see a thing. We can only hear what seems to be an epic battle being fought around the trucks. No one dares to move or peek out of the truck. What can you do in a moment like this but pray? *God*, I begin, *you know why we have come on this journey. You know the heart of everyone here. Please don't subject us to this.*

When the shouting and shooting stop, a driver appears. He tells us that two of the three trucks and their passengers have been taken as hostages. This is not an uncommon scenario, unfortunately. When migrants are taken as hostages, they are told that they must contact their families—their poor families who already shoulder so much debt—and come up with a ransom fee if they want to be released. It's one of many common dangers along the migrant route. Those of us in the truck with the ruptured gas tank? We are lucky. The truck I feared so much just a few hours ago has actually been our blessing—the only reason it wasn't held for ransom is because of the broken tank. There wasn't enough gas for the kidnappers to take us hostage. It wasn't worth it for them, and so we escaped. I am stunned by this harsh miracle, by the series of small choices we make freely and, especially, the ones that we are forced to make, and how they each serve to move us out of harm's way.

The driver tells us we are in Michoacán. This Mexican state is famous for many things, especially avocados, monarch butterflies, and drug cartels. We have survived the most recent threat, but relief is not in sight. We still have no food and no water, and we are exhausted, but we have to sleep in the truck. We have all basically turned into cadavers. The only difference between us and the dead is that we are breathing.

This is the point in the trip when all of us in the group begin to feel the strain, and in my mind, it's the most tenuous moment of our journey because internal discord among people with a common cause can be more devastating than any other danger. We each become selfish, concerned about our own comfort, about our own survival, rather than the greater good of our group. Everyone tries, at some point, to claim a bit more space for themselves, and an outstretched leg can provoke a heated outburst from someone who feels their miniscule territory in the truck is being invaded.

The same bits of conversation are uttered again and again— I'm hot; I'm thirsty; I can't see a thing; I can't feel my legs— the refrains so obvious and so worn out that they are grating on the ears. Even the most likable person becomes unbearably annoying. Children's hunger and boredom become constant flash points, as parents try to soothe and comfort them with little more than words and a caress. When Fernando asks how much longer the trip is going to take, I say that we're on vacation, and we haven't arrived at our destination just yet.

"Isn't this quite the adventure?" I ask him. Although I am exhausted, I force myself to smile and to ask the question with cheerfulness in my voice. He looks at me dolefully and shakes his head.

"I don't like this vacation," he says solemnly, in a sad tone I've never heard from him before.

———

On a trip like this, you are never in control. You don't know where, when, or what you will eat—or whether you will eat at all. You don't know when you will be able to stop and enjoy the feeling of a rush of blood circulating through your legs, as you lift and shake each one to make sure you can still walk. You don't know when you will be able to sleep, though you can be certain you will never sleep well. And you are definitely not in control of when and where you will be able to go to the bathroom, although you can be sure it will never happen when you actually *need* to relieve yourself. Of course, this is all exponentially more challenging to bear if you are traveling with children.

Since the bandits took two of the three trucks in Michoacán, my sense of fear has increased. So, too, has my sense of awareness. Though the trip is taking its toll on me, I know from my previous journey that I have to pace myself. I can't waste all of my physical and emotional energy now if I want us to make it to the finish line. I must remain alert at all times, especially because

I am a woman traveling with children. Men will do bad things to a woman who is vulnerable. They'll flirt or feel her up, at best. At worst, they'll rape her. That happens to too many migrant women along their journeys. Many of us get shots or buy birth control pills at a local pharmacy or on the black market before we leave home. Other than that, what can we do? Nothing. We are entirely in their hands. The only thing we can do is ensure that we never let our guard down because violations against a woman's safety occur when a man perceives an opportunity he can take advantage of.

It's for this reason that I never want to let Yordy or Fernando out of my sight. People know that a woman with children is easier to harm. Threaten her kids, and you can achieve whatever you desire, because she will do anything—and they know this—to protect her children. This is why I always keep my boys close. But there are rare moments when I have to take my eyes off them for a split second—like when I need to use the bathroom and actually have the chance to do so.

After the truck hostage incident, we head deeper into Michoacán. At some point, the truck slows and then stops, and we're told to get out; we have a few minutes to stretch and turn our faces to the sun. The timing is just right for me—I need to relieve myself. I scramble down an embankment, my children just beyond my line of sight. I pull my pants down, I squat, I wait for that moment of relief, which is so rare on these trips. As I'm finishing, I turn my head and see a human skeleton on the ground next to me. Horror washes over me, and I feel dizzy. *God, be with me. God, be with us. God, were you with this person when they met their end? What were they fleeing? What were they seeking? What led to this moment when their body was tossed over an embankment, another anonymous body joining the ones whose bones are littered all over this land?*

I am overcome with terror and disgust, and my stomach churns. Our own drivers could just throw us out and leave us here. I pull my pants up as fast as I can and scramble up the hill, heaving a sigh of relief when I see my boys there, safe.

6

Arrival

The eight days and nights you spend in the truck leave you debilitated in every way: emotionally, spiritually, physically. By the time you reach the Mexico-US border, nearly 2,300 miles later, you are tapping into your last reserves. But some people have almost nothing left. They've come this whole, horrible way, only to have the border in sight and no will left to run for it and reach it. Of course, this is compounded by the fact that the people who you have paid to bring you this far want to attempt one last effort to make money off of you.

Before our drivers urge us onward to the border, they ask all of us whether we have money, phones, or jewelry. If we do, they say, we should leave these items with them because if ICE catches us and finds these on our person, we will be held for a longer period of time. Because I have been through this before, I know that this isn't true. I know that our phones can be used for evidence, but money and jewelry will have no impact on how long we are held in detention. For this reason, I keep the 200 Mexican pesos I have left tucked out of sight, resting underneath one of my breasts, inside my bra, the secret safe of every woman migrant.

Others don't know that what the drivers say is untrue, however, and they are so weary that they unlatch their necklaces or hand over whatever cash they have left. I imagine the drivers in the truck an hour from now, sorting through their loot and guffawing at the innocence of these vulnerable people they have just scammed successfully, and with the greatest of ease.

As we approach the border, I prepare myself mentally. In my mind, it's not just my responsibility to make sure that my children and I cross safely. I also want to support those who have made this journey with us. Some people, when they get to the last part of the trip, just break, with fear, uncertainty—something paralyzes them. We are yards from the border and I know: we have to run, we have to run NOW. I say this to the ones who are just standing there, dumbstruck. "RUN. RUN NOW!" I urge them, with a voice that's dry and hoarse from dehydration. But some can't. They are pale, frozen, unable to move.

I realize with horror that my own child is one of them. Yordy is exhausted. He is also overweight; he simply has more body to move. I can tell that he is barely conscious. I look at his eyes, his mouth. His face has changed. Yes, the truck was full of moments that were tense and tiring and terrifying. But now we're HERE. It's time to move. This is it. This is the singular moment we've been waiting for, the goal we've been moving toward for the days we have agonized in the back of that truck. But the soil is sandy; it's so hard to lift your feet, to put one foot in front of the other. Yordy thinks he's moving, but he's not. This is my son. I can't run and leave him now. He's the whole reason we're making this journey. I have to hang back and motivate him.

"Look," I say to him, gently but with urgency, pointing to the goal. "It's so close." I have Fernando under one arm. I lock eyes with Yordy. Everyone else has crossed. We are still on the Mexican side of the border. We have to go. NOW. "*Vamos*, Yordy!" I say. And we begin to run.

A canal full of water stands between us and the United States. We have watched people jump over the canal or into it. Coyotes use this section of the border, in San Luis, Arizona, to cross people over because it has only the canal and low wooden fencing that acts as a vehicle barrier dividing the two countries. Comparatively speaking, it's a much easier crossing than "the wall." The nearly twenty-foot-high sections of the wall aren't far away, but they pose a much more challenging entry point, so coyotes avoid them. People trying desperately to climb the wall have fallen off it and broken multiple bones or worse. Seven months after we entered the United States, a Guatemalan woman was impaled when she fell off the wall and onto a piece of rebar that pierced her buttock and her torso. Those kinds of stories turn your stomach, especially when you realize that the part of the border you will cross depends entirely upon the guides who have been paid to bring you here. The wall is an especially hard place to cross for migrants with children or people with disabilities.

On the other side of the canal, we can see US Border Patrol trucks and Border Patrol agents yelling, "No, don't jump!" They have life preservers that they throw out to you if you can't scramble up the steep side of the canal. They save you, but it's not a humanitarian gesture. It's just part of the job. Border Patrol agents grab us as we're descending into the canal. Later, I'll be grateful that we didn't make it into the water, which would have left us with an unbearable chill.

The agents catch us and ask us where we are from. They pull our shoelaces out of our shoes immediately and take hair bands out of our hair. Even though it's hard to believe, the hair bands and shoelaces can be used as weapons. The Border Patrol agents take our bags, whatever we have left, though by this time, most of us have gotten rid of everything. They give us an alien number. Then, they throw us in a fenced area we call the dog pound or a holding cell called the icebox—so named because it is freezing in there. Whatever objects we've managed to save are put in bags and marked with our names.

A girl who had jumped into the water is shivering, her clothes soaked through. I realize that they're not going to give her a dry change of clothes. They're going to dump her in the icebox like that. My heart aches for her. She doesn't matter to them. The agents don't even notice her. She's just one of so many, a problem for them to solve quickly before moving on to the next one. To them, we are all just one big mass of a problem; none of us is an individual person with stories and fears, hopes, dreams, and plans.

This experience is markedly different from my arrival with

Fernando in 2014. Back then, yes, we were apprehended and taken into custody by ICE. But it's shocking to me how much things have changed in so little time. Four years ago, the officers were doing their jobs, but they also expressed concern about our well-being. "Are you cold?" they asked, and if we said, "Yes," they brought us a real blanket, not an oversize sheet of aluminum foil. "Are you hungry?" they asked, and if we said, "Yes," they brought us something to eat, a snack at least. They told us to lie down and rest, to recover from the trip; and they checked on us regularly, asking us how we felt and whether we were okay. They seemed to care, even if they were just doing their jobs.

Back then, when we were released, we were taken to a luxurious house, where a woman told us to make ourselves at home. I still don't understand this; I still don't know who she was. It all seemed like a dream. She showed us the refrigerator, which was stuffed full of food, and told us we could eat anything we wanted. She showed us to our beds—they were so comfortable!—and told us to rest. She said she had to go out for the evening, but she'd be back the next day and we should settle in as if this were our house. I couldn't sleep a wink—the whole situation was so strange, and I was suspicious—but I was grateful all the same.

But this time, things are clearly going to be different; I can see that right away. Not a single one of the officers seems to care whether we are cold or hungry, whether we are tired or uncomfortable. In fact, they don't seem to care about us at all. Early on, I know we are in for a very different, very hard experience. I just don't know how different or hard it will be.

7

The Icebox

In the icebox, we wait for our turn to give our information to ICE officials. When my name is called, agents ask me who accompanied me, and I say, "My two sons, Yordy and Fernando." They ask for our complete names, dates of birth, and the like— and they ask why we are entering their country. I explain our situation, and they waste no time in telling us that we shouldn't be here, that we are going to be deported, that our trip was a waste of time and money. I say nothing. If there is anything I've learned in life, it's that sometimes, silence is better and more effective than an outspoken response.

When I refuse to placate them with more information or to react to their insults, the officers tell me that we are going to be moved to cells, where we will wait. I tell them this is fine. But then they tell me that Yordy is going to one cell and Fernando and I are going to another. My heart skips a beat, and I find the courage to say, "He is my son. He's coming with me."

"No," the officer says in an implacable voice. "He's going to another cell because he's a big boy." He says "big boy" with a sneer, like he knows that Yordy is a mama's boy, which, of course, means a weak boy.

"He's a minor," I reply. The officer insists that Yordy must go to a different cell, where other boys his age are being held. I realize, with resignation, how utterly powerless I am. I look at Yordy and tell him that this separation will be for only a few hours, that I'll see him soon, and that I love him. I try to stay strong, but I am full of questions. I am dying to know what is going to happen to him, and I'm crushed by the fact that I won't be there by his side to protect him.

The guards escort Fernando and me to a different cell, which already has fifteen or more women inside it. Some of them have one or two children with them. Everyone is cold and desperate, the smell of fear thick on their bodies. Some of them are trying to rest on old, thin cushions that can't rightfully be called mattresses. Other people are lying on the frigid floor because they are so exhausted. They shiver uncontrollably.

The cell is crowded for its size. I find a place to sit on the corner of a freezing bench, and I try to cover Fernando with a little blanket, which the agents would consider contraband. A few of our cell mates are lucky enough to be wearing sweaters. Others say that they have a sweater in their backpack, and they are hoping the agents will allow them to retrieve these so they can ward off the chill of the icebox. "*Oficial*, may we get our sweaters?" they ask. The answer, of course, is no. The cold seems exacerbated by the deliberate cruelty.

Every few minutes, I get up from the bench and walk to the window. I press my face against it, trying to see whether I can spot Yordy so that I can communicate without words that we are here, he is there, and that everything will be okay. I look and look, straining my eyes. But I can't see him.

My neck aches, and with every passing moment, it throbs with an increasingly insistent pain. An officer comes around distributing instant soups for everyone, soups that are cold and undercooked, the noodles still hard. I ask, "Could I possibly get some pain medication, please? My neck hurts terribly." The officer denies my request, saying that I can receive help only if there is an emergency and I need to go to the hospital. "You just have to deal with the pain," he says.

Months from now, when there are news stories about children dying in the icebox, I won't be surprised. The conditions in the icebox don't support life, especially for a baby or young child, even though the officers say the cold is for our own good. According to them, maintaining a low temperature in the icebox helps ward off or kill the contagious illnesses that can flourish in cramped spaces. But the cold itself can kill, especially if your body is weak from your journey.

In the icebox, you are completely subject to the will of immigration officials. You never know whether it's day or night—you can't see outside. You can't feed your child when he wants to eat. You can't read to him or encourage him to play with a toy because no personal items are allowed unless you've managed to somehow sneak something in and keep it from the guards' view. You can't reply to any of his questions—Why are we here? When will we leave? When will I see my big brother?—because you don't know the answers. You can't tuck him in and make him comfortable because the only space left for him to sleep in the overcrowded cell is on your lap.

You don't even have power over your own body. You can't bathe at your leisure. There in the icebox I can't bear the feeling of filth anymore, so I break the monotony by trying to wash my hair in the cell's small sink. I beg some of the women who have babies to give me some wet wipes so I can clean the rest of my body and so I can wipe Fernando down, too. They are so kind to share the wipes with me, and I rub the damp cloths over our skin: face, arms and hands, private parts. We aren't free, but at least we feel a bit refreshed.

Three days later, I finally see Yordy for the first time. Seventy-two hours can feel like a lifetime, especially when you're sitting in a cold cell, anxious and afraid, with nothing to do but think. We spot each other through a window, our eyes meeting. I am so desperate to hold him, to embrace him, but I can't. So, I just ask God to give us the strength to overcome this excruciatingly painful moment. I wonder how he is feeling, what he is thinking. I wonder whether he is able to sleep and whether he is eating. These are a mother's concerns for her child. Yordy is my oldest, my first child. He made me a mother. Because of that, and because of his father's death, I have always felt an extra special protectiveness toward him. In the icebox, unable to do anything for him or to know how he is, I have been in a state of anxiety unlike anything I've ever known.

Two more days pass, and ICE officials finally call me to fill out paperwork. They ask me for all of our information again—names, dates of birth, country of origin—and I wonder why we are required to provide details we've already given so many times. Are they trying to catch us in a lie? Or are they really that disorganized? Either way, I allow myself the small indulgence of thinking that completing more paperwork is a good sign. I think to myself, *Soon, we will be together again.* But my hopes are dashed when, upon finishing the paperwork, they take me back to the frigid icebox. More difficult than anything else is not knowing what is happening, what will happen next. It is more difficult than being hungry, more difficult than being cold.

The next day, I'm called out of the cell again. An officer asks me whether anyone in the United States can receive my children.

"No," I reply, "I don't have any family in this country." It is an honest answer, the only answer. It is also an answer that changes everything.

"Your kids can't stay in this facility any longer," the officer replies, talking at me without meeting my gaze. "We're going to send them to a better place while we process your paperwork."

A better place? There is no better place for a child than being with its mother! My mind, which has been so vacant and quiet, is suddenly tormented with a whirlwind of thoughts and questions, questions that I know the officer won't answer. *When will they take my children? Where? For how long? Who will take care of them? When will I see them again?* The officer won't say, offers no information at all. I don't want my kids to leave here without me.

Back in the cell, I cradle Fernando on my lap, worry gnawing at my mind and heart. He seems to have a stomach virus, probably because of the water and the cold soup. He's retching, his small body doubling over as he strains to vomit. His forehead feels clammy when I stroke it. Maybe it's better if he is taken somewhere else. At the very least, it might be a warmer place, one where he can have some hot food. Since we have already been here for nearly a week, I think that whatever paperwork needs to be finished should be done within a couple of days, so fine: take the boys somewhere warmer, and I will see them again in two or three days.

How innocent the mind can be! Nothing could have prepared me for what came next.

8

Separation

The day after the officer tells me my boys are going to be taken to a better facility, another officer calls out my name. The rough voice cuts through my dream; all of us in the cell are sleeping, or attempting to anyway. I try to get up from the floor without waking Fernando, and I walk toward the cell door. "Bring your son," the officer says. I turn and bend down to scoop him up in my arms, careful not to disturb his sleep. He isn't wearing any shoes.

"Take him to the bathroom and clean him up," the officer barks. "They're going to take him now, and he needs to be washed before he goes."

"I need to go back to the cell, please," I answer. "I need to get his shoes and his dinosaur." Fernando had brought his stuffed dinosaur toy all the way from Guatemala. Thousands of miles and a million bumps and switchbacks from home, the olive-colored T-Rex, complete with claws and a full set of menacing teeth, is still with him. We have managed not to lose it, always careful to make sure it is with us. The dinosaur helps him sleep and, truth be told, has become his faithful friend, a creature to whom he can confess his worries and fears, and in which he can seek comfort. When he needs to be strong, he roars like a dinosaur.

"You can't take anything out of the cell now," the officer responds, pointing me toward the bathroom. I'm confused and afraid, a giant knot of sorrow forming in my throat. I spot Yordy outside his cell area; he's also being directed to the showers. I run to him and wrap him in an embrace, waking Fernando up in the process. Yordy and I are crying, and he's asking me, "Ma, what's going to happen?"

Fernando, shaking off sleep, looks at us wide-eyed. "What's happening?" he asks.

"Nothing," I say, in the calmest tone I can muster. "I'm going to give you a shower so that you can go out for a walk with Yordy."

Fernando is still sleepy and he is young, but he is not stupid. "And you?" he asks. "Are you coming with us?"

I try to find the right words and force them up and around the knot in my throat. "I'll come along later," I manage to say. "I have to take care of a few things here, so I'll come behind you in a little while. Besides, we can't all fit in the car." I wash him as the water streams from the showerhead, a cascade that reminds me of tears. I hold back my own cries. I don't want the boys to know how much I am suffering, how scared I am.

We all step out of the shower area, and the boys are given

gray sweat suits, which they are told to put on. Then, they are handed a pair of flip-flops. Fernando's are too large, and his feet can't control them. No one bothers to look for a pair that will fit him, and so they take off the flip-flops and leave him like that, without any shoes at all. He's not even wearing socks.

————

The boys are dressed, and so it is time to say goodbye. We hug each other tightly, and I tell Yordy that he has to take care of Fernando and that we will see one another again very soon. He is weeping. Fernando, confused, has his arms locked around Yordy's neck. I watch them be led away.

How much I want to run and go with them! When they are out of my sight, I can't hold my tears back any longer; I cry and cry and cry. All I want to do is collapse on the floor and weep until my body has released all of its tears. Instead, the officer tells me that I need to take whatever I have in the cell and bring it with me. I'm moving, too.

I see a clock and take note of the time: it's 2 a.m. The officers have taken my children in the middle of the night! I grab Fernando's little shoes, his dinosaur, and his blanket. The officer shows me to another cell, and I'm locked in. Looking around, it takes me no time at all to realize who this cell is for. There are no children in the cell. We are all mothers here, mothers whose children have been taken from them.

The next day, I cry without ceasing. Who knew the body could produce so many tears? They don't offer relief, though; the more I cry, the more pain I feel. Another mother approaches me, leaning down and touching my arm gently. "Calm down now, calm down," she says. I know she is trying to help me, and that she understands the pain I am feeling because it is also her pain, but the suffering is so profound that her words have no effect.

9

Lockup

The road from San Luis to Eloy Detention Center is not a straight one. From the icebox, a group of us is transported in what migrants call the *perrera*, the dog catcher's truck, because that's exactly what it looks like. We are driven more than three and a half hours to the east, to the Florence Correctional Center. We spend several hours there, waiting in a trailer, though we don't know for what, since no one ever bothers to explain anything to us. This constant silence, the lack of information, the treatment of us as if we simply aren't here is maddening.

Later, we're put on a bus and driven south, to a facility called Santa Cruz. It sits right on the border at Nogales, like San Luis. Sometimes now, I'll look at a map on the internet and see the vast spaces we covered, noticing that between these southernmost points of the Arizona border, there's a national monument with a beautiful name—Organ Pipe Cactus. Maybe I'll go there someday and see the cacti; I've read it is the only place it grows naturally in the wild. In the borderland space between San Luis and Nogales, there is also a large Indian reservation, which, I've read, has some tribal members who live here, in the United States, and some who live in northern Mexico. The border divides their land—a wound, a scar, a bridge. They oppose the wall, even though their tribal members have special permission from both the US and Mexican governments to cross back and forth. The towns on this part of the map have names that sound as if they could be on a map of Guatemala: Tat Momoli, Comobabi, Tumacácori-Carmen.

At the Santa Cruz detention center, we are told that our final destination is going to be Eloy, an ICE detention center to the north of here, but they can't take us there just yet. The facility is completely full, a prison full of migrant women, most of them forcibly separated from their children at the border. After a week, we're told to form a single-file line, and we're led back to a bus, this time bound for Eloy. When we get there, we are given our prison jumpsuits and taken to our cells.

For close to eighty days, this is my home.

————

A strange moment occurs during the first few weeks I'm locked up, when I've managed to exert some control over the initial gut punch of fear and uncertainty and when my body has had a chance to begin recovering from the dehydration and exhaustion of the trip from Guatemala. It's a shared moment that descends upon me suddenly when I'm sitting in the recreation area with some other women, working on a jigsaw puzzle.

As we separate straight-edge pieces from the interior pieces, which will all be joined to make an image of a map of the United States, we look at the shape of each state and sound out the names of the ones where we plan to live. "MEE-SI-SEE-PEE." "NORT-CAR-O-LINE-AH." "NOO-JORK." One woman interrupts our pronunciation game with a small laugh. "Isn't it funny?" she asks, snapping a piece of the border into place. "In a way, we don't have to worry about anything here! This morning, I didn't have to worry about going to find something to eat, nor to find wood to cook with. I didn't have to worry about what clothes to wear—we're all wearing the same ugly thing!" Laughter ripples through the group as we all take stock of each other's coarse, ugly jumpsuits, which are ill-fitting, obscuring each woman's form and her individual style.

I try to imagine how each woman might dress and accessorize herself outside the bars and walls and barbed wire, and I match her personality with a certain look. To play this imaginary dress-up-doll type of game, I think about the clothes and jewelry and accessories I sold in my shop. This woman, I think, probably wears colorful leggings and a blouse with some sparkly sequins and platform wedge sandals. She carries one of those small purses that has a metal chain for a strap, and she likes big earrings and bangles on her wrists. That woman, though, is much more conservative. She wears longer skirts and modest tops, trying not to draw too much attention to herself. If she wears jewelry at all, it's a simple gold chain, and she keeps her money folded up in a pocket or apron she ties tightly around her waist. Her shoes are simple sandals.

My mind wanders like this for a few minutes and then comes back to the puzzle and the conversation. "For the first time in my life, I'm not running here and there, here and there, to make money, or take care of my kids, or to do anything!" another woman says. "When was the last time any of you sat around and did nothing at all? How long has it been since you sat down and worked on a puzzle?"

"Never!" says another *compañera*, as she shakes her head.

"How long has it been since I've just sat down and drawn a picture?" yet another woman wonders aloud. She thinks about it for a minute, before admitting that she can't actually remember. Maybe never.

The conversation started with a humorous tone and has left us in a companionable, convivial silence as we keep sorting puzzle pieces, but I can't help but reflect more deeply upon the women's words and observations. For the first time in our lives, we aren't working ourselves to the bone. We think we are indispensable, that we are so needed, but the sobering realization that descends upon me here in detention is that we are not. Our children have been taken from us, and someone else is taking care of them. That doesn't mean we don't want to be caring for them, or that we are experiencing this relaxing moment of putting a puzzle together as if we were all on a girlfriends' vacation.

For me, it's a moment for us to meditate on what we really want out of life and what we have to offer. Outside this detention center, life hurtles along, and our families are learning to live without us. It is hard to think about this, but it's also necessary to do so. I take a deep breath and say a silent prayer: *God, I don't know where my children are or who they're with, but I know they are in your hands, so I trust you. Show me the reason that you have for me to be here.* And over time, He does. He shows me that the world is the world, and it's going to keep spinning whether I'm here or not, so I have to work on my spiritual life. What had I done to nurture my spiritual life before Eloy? Nothing.

———

Detention offers plenty of opportunities to deepen one's spiritual life, that's for sure. In a setting where boredom and deprivation reign, it's easy for even the most centered person to lose her temper or find a problem she isn't looking for. Petty fights are everyday occurrences.

Bunkies squabble, for example, over the square foot–size window in their cell and who has access to its view of the men's detention facility, which is just barely visible across the yard. Our windows are laminated with a polarized film and have bars, but that doesn't stop women from crowding onto the top bunk to look for a little action. They jockey with one another for the chance to press a paper with a handwritten message up against the window, as if any man looking through a similar window from so far away could possibly read their declarations of love and lust. They make absurd claims on men whose features they can barely make out and whose character they certainly can't assess from this distance. "He's MY man!" "Woman, what are you talking about? Are you crazy? Do you want a problem with me? He's MY man!"

Women who might be perfect angels on the street will open their tops and press their breasts against the window, putting on a show that they hope will be reciprocated, waiting and watching to see what they can see, hoping for any kind of diversion to distinguish today from yesterday and tomorrow. I stay on the bottom bunk and listen as my cell mate narrates the day's action, shaking my head and not wanting any part of it.

Eventually, the daily peep shows become so problematic that the guards bring all of us together and give us a stern lecture. They tell us that we are prohibited from showing any body parts to the male detainees. They threaten us with a story of a woman they've thrown in solitary confinement, or the hole, for such behavior. "If you want to avoid a similar fate," they say in a serious voice, with their eyes narrowed and foreheads furrowed, "you'd better stop showing off your breasts."

———

I've never pressed my breasts against the glass, and I have no interest in doing so. But the thing is, even when you're doing everything you can to avoid trouble, it has no problem finding you. My conflict—the one that puts my spiritual development project to the test so that God can see just how ready and willing I am to let Him mold me—is over something as simple as a Styrofoam cup-a-soup.

The lines for the microwave are always long, not only because there are so many women for just one microwave, but also because the cup-a-soup from commissary takes fifteen minutes to heat. It's not a practical meal for people in prison. Fifteen minutes is plenty of time for a problem to erupt.

I'm next in line for the microwave. The machine has beeped to indicate that the soup of the woman who is in front of me has finished cooking, but she's nowhere to be seen. "Whose soup is this?" I ask. No one answers. Someone calls out, "Patel! Patel! Your soup is done!" but Patel, an eighteen-year-old girl from India, doesn't come to claim the soup, and the line of women behind me is getting restless. My bunkie speaks up: "Rosy, just take Patel's soup out of the microwave and set it aside so we can all eat sometime today!" I open the door, take the soup out, and set it on the table. I put my soup in and turn the dial to the fifteen-minute mark.

As soon as the machine sputters back to life, Patel shows up. When she sees her soup on the table, she's keyed up and ready to fight. She grabs the door of the microwave and yanks it open. She pulls out my soup, which was given to me by a friend, and throws it on the floor. The square block of still hard noodles shatters, scattering across the floor as the water from the Styrofoam cup pools at my feet.

She screams something at me, but we don't share a language. I try to explain through pantomime that the microwave had already stopped. She yells at me again and gestures at my Bible; I can imagine her saying something like, "What good does it do you to walk around with your Bible tucked under your arm and act all self-righteous and pious when you're such a liar?"

God, be with me, I think. It's clear to me that she wants to fight, but I won't give it to her. God is working on me, giving me a chance to change my character. Patel is God in disguise, giving me an opportunity to practice self-control and patience.

It's an important lesson to learn because if there are any characteristics one needs in detention, it's these: self-control and patience.

The days and weeks drag by. The hardest part is not knowing how long I will be here, and although I'm grateful for the time to nurture my relationship with God and focus wholly on Him, I'd be lying if I didn't admit that I also feel restless sometimes.

There are occasional moments of happiness, such as the days, about once a week, when I get to speak to Yordy and Fernando. "We are okay, Ma," Yordy tells me, assuring me that he is taking good care of Fernando. They live in a part of New York City called the Bronx, and they are staying with a Spanish-speaking foster mother who is kind to them and feeds them well. Several other boys who were also taken from their mothers at the border are living in the same apartment with the same foster mother—

eight in all. Yordy says he knows of another foster family that's housing thirteen boys.

So many children without their parents!, I think to myself. I wonder where *their* mothers are, and whether they are locked up here with me. I wonder how they fill their days as they wait to be reunited with their children.

Each morning, Yordy says, their foster mother wakes them up, lays out their clothes for them, gives them breakfast, and herds them out to her van, driving them across the bridge and into Manhattan, where they spend the day at a place called Cayuga Centers. It's the foster-care agency that placed them with the woman who is caring for them. Many months from now, I'll learn that this center, like another one called Southwest Key, has made millions of dollars in profit off of caring for our children—a fact that makes activists suspicious of them, compelling them to hold protests outside of these centers. But Yordy assures me that his foster mother and the Cayuga caseworkers are all good people and that he and Fernando will be safe until we are reunited. I hope what he's saying is true.

In the afternoon, the foster mother picks the boys up again and takes them home to her apartment, which sits above a deli that's across the street from a playground that's part of one of the city's big housing projects. She isn't supposed to let them out of her sight, he says, but she lets them go to the playground without her because she trusts the older boys to watch the younger ones. She calls them all "*mi hijo*," "my son," but if they are tempted to call her "*Mamá*," she makes sure that they add her name afterward. She doesn't want them to confuse her with their biological mothers. She's not looking to replace anyone, she says. She's just holding the boys in a safe and loving embrace until we are reunited.

When the boys ask her when that might be, she is honest and says that she doesn't know. She assures them that their mothers love them and that we would come back right this second if we could. She also has her own biological children, though they are grown. She knows the heart of a mother. When I speak with the boys, Yordy also asks when I am coming back and I say, "Soon," even though I have no idea when we will be together again. "*Primero Dios*," I tell him. "Pray to God every day that we will be reunited when He is ready. Don't lose faith." He says he trusts me and that he trusts God, and he knows we will be reunited soon.

———

Detention also makes you clever. With a lack of, well, everything—except time to kill—you quickly discover how creative human beings are—how creative *you* are—how we can all see a need and fill it with just a bit of inventiveness. You learn how to heat a cold, tasteless tortilla on the faucet of a prison cell sink by running the hot water for five minutes until it's scorching, or how to whiten your socks and undergarments by using toothpaste since you don't have bleach.

Being locked up makes you see with new eyes. It leads you to discover abilities and skills you didn't know you had. Trash bags become homemade rosaries, complete with all fifty-nine beads and Jesus writhing on the crucifix in the agonizing throes of death.

One woman here marries a man who is also in detention—somehow, they managed to secure a visit and have a marriage ceremony approved to sanctify their union—and someone fashions wedding bands for them out of plastic cutlery. The rings are even inscribed with their names!

A large number of women pass the time making magic by weaving empty potato chip bags, which would otherwise be destined for the garbage bin, into attractive, colorful wallets or purses. There's certainly no shortage of supplies for this craft, and at Eloy, detained craftswomen trade these handmade treasures for commissary goods or phone time. They barter and haggle as if they were at their local market—"I'll give you this purse I made if you promise me ten Maruchan soups." Later, on the outside, I'll learn that purses and bags like these sell at chic stores for an absurd amount of money—$20 at a minimum, but hundreds of dollars in some cases.

We also express our creativity and resourcefulness when it's time to mark milestones and celebrations, such as birthdays or releases, which are happening more frequently because of the activist mothers and their fundraising, or when we want to show our gratitude. One woman detained here has helped many of us write bond hearing letters, and Dalila, a Mexican woman who has a talent for making interesting things out of nothing, declares that she will make this woman a cake as a communal thank-you from all of us.

Dalila is bold, and she manages to steal a few eggs from the chow hall. She enlists some of us to take the bread from our meals, to flatten the yeasty rolls and press them into napkins, and then to stuff the ropelike contraband into our bras to avoid detection when the guards conduct their pat-down inspections. She obliges other detainees into service, too, encouraging them to hoard butter and powdered coffee creamer. We smuggle these items out of the cafeteria and back to our cells and then make sure they get passed to Dalila in her cell. Somehow, without a bowl or a whisk or an oven, without flour or vanilla, she whips all these contraband ingredients into an impressive cake, with icing and everything.

The sweetness isn't just from the ingredients; it's from her creativity and effort, which make the cake better than any store-bought card or gift.

———

The celebratory moments, though, are few and far between. Most days are characterized by a mind- and soul-numbing dullness. In Eloy, we have nothing. We have no one but ourselves. We don't have money. We aren't the owners of our own lives or destinies. We can't decide when we wake up. We can't decide when we go to bed. We can't decide whether or when we want to bathe. We have nothing, nothing but God.

For those of us who considered ourselves women of faith before—and that is most of us—we have become more fervent. Eloy is a revelation, a tight blindfold pulled from our eyes. Detention, oddly, is an amazing grace. Once, we were blind; now, we are beginning to see. Slowly, often painfully, we begin to realize that what we require to survive exists inside ourselves and in our relationship with God. We realize that material things are largely unimportant. In the moment in our lives when we are least free, in the literal sense, many of us finally discover freedom.

10

Takeoff and Landing

"Pack it up, Pablo Cruz," La Miss says, as if I actually have something to pack other than my Bible and Fernando's little stuffed dinosaur, which I've managed to save. What does she mean, exactly? Am I leaving my bunkie, Lucrecia, to change cells, and if so, why? I think back to the visit with José Orochena two days ago. He had said he thought I'd be released, but even though I had allowed myself a bit of hope, I hadn't placed my faith in that possibility. But could it be? Am I leaving Eloy?

I am! And although I am elated—maybe I'll see my boys soon!—I am also overcome by other emotions, including sadness. When women are released from Eloy, they are never given enough time to say goodbye to anyone. Despite all the bickering and squabbling that define day-to-day life in a detention center, intense friendships are also formed; the shared experiences of separation and deprivation create a special sisterhood. This is especially true for bunkies because they spend long periods of time together. I will miss many women here, but Lucrecia especially. The fact that we are both from Guatemala, that we both had children taken away from us, that we both have a deep faith, and, of course, the space we shared—it all made for a close relationship, and I hate to leave her behind, especially without knowing what her own future might hold.

José has flown in from New York to pick me up at Eloy. As the gates swing open and I feel the desert heat enfold me, I notice that he is dressed in the same suit and same jaunty hat that he wore on the day we met. I'm in a state of shock and feel as if I've been swept up into the vortex of a tornado, with everyone and everything whirling around me with such speed that I can't distinguish any of it clearly. The tears welling up in my eyes and spilling down my cheeks make things blurry, too.

How does life change so quickly? One moment, you're sitting in a cell in a detention center, waiting for time to pass. The next, you're taking off your prison uniform and putting on your street clothes, the ones you wore on your journey from your country to the United States. They haven't been washed, of course, and they no longer fit because you've lost so much weight. One moment, the people in charge of you treat you with apathy or outright disgust. The next, you discover people with enormous smiles and open arms who are waiting for you, people you don't even know, who take your hand and tell you that everything is going to be all right, and that they're going to walk with you on this next part of your life's journey.

———

José opens the passenger door of the SUV he has rented and I get into the car. Floridalma and Lilian, two other women for whom bond has been posted, get into the back seat. Their children were also taken from them. One is from Guatemala; the other, Honduras. We talk a bit among ourselves, sharing disbelief that we are finally free. We talk about our families, where they are and whether our children are still in foster care. A lot has happened since we were all detained; Floridalma's oldest daughter, for instance, has just had a baby, making Floridalma a grandmother for the first time.

José slips into the driver's seat and starts the engine. The detention center recedes from our view and we stop just beyond its periphery, where a group of reporters is waiting for us. "How do you feel?" asks one white reporter in Spanish. It is difficult to answer him; none of us has the words to explain anything just yet, especially to people who haven't lived what we have gone through.

We drive on to a department store called JCPenney, where José says he wants to buy us some clothes and shoes. He can see plainly that the clothes we have on are soiled and ill-fitting, and he wants us to be comfortable as we each set off on separate cross-country trips to reunite with our families. As for the shoes, ICE returned to us the shoes that we were wearing when we arrived in the United States but didn't return the shoelaces. Those are long gone. I imagine that somewhere in an ICE office a closet contains an enormous mound of shoelaces, a tangle of black, white, blue, red, and brown, long laces and short ones, pulled from the shoes of parents and their children.

Walking around without shoelaces bears a particular humili-
ation because it's not normal. Even if someone doesn't know that
our lack of shoelaces is a sign of having been in detention, the
awkward way one walks when one's shoes have no laces draws
attention and sets one apart as being different: poor, unkempt,
someone who doesn't take care of themselves or their appearance. Others look at your shoes, they look at you, and they express a kind of pity. I will be so grateful for a new pair of shoes.

As we shop, lifting blouses and pants or skirts off the racks to
hold them up and assess whether they might fit the bodies that
changed so much during detention, a woman rushes over to us
with three small gift bags in her hand. José told her a little bit
about our story while we were shopping, and she felt so moved
that she hurried to choose some items for us from the Sephora
cosmetics counter. She offers us the bags with both hands, saying
that her father had been a Customs and Border Patrol officer.
I'm struck by the irony, but moved by her gesture, and I thank
her over and over again.

"I'm so sorry for what you all are going through," she says,
and I feel that she really means it. She is the first person to offer
this kind of apology, but she won't be the last. In the days ahead,
many people will tell me they are sorry for what their country is
putting immigrants through. Some of them will even ask me to
forgive them, as if I am a priest who can grant divine absolution
to wipe away the stain of someone's sins.

We each choose some clothes and a pair of shoes, and we
walk to the register with José. I've picked out a pair of blue pants

and black Nike tennis shoes. I'm grateful but nervous, still not wholly believing that someone would give so much without the expectation of eventual return. Is José *sure* I won't have to repay the $12,000 bond or whatever these nice clothes cost? On our way to the department store, José had passed around his cell phone, telling us to call whomever we wanted, even family members back in our home countries. I called my sister Elvira, who couldn't believe I was calling from a phone outside the detention center. I kept the call short, but we cried together, and it was the most special moment for my family and me. As I reflect on everything that's happening, I can't imagine how I could even begin to compensate for so much generosity.

José places our shopping bags in the trunk and drives onward to a hotel near Phoenix. There, more volunteers receive us with a warm welcome and show us to our rooms. They tell us to take our time and freshen up; later, we'll meet again and go out for dinner. For the first time in months, I feel free to take a bath without someone timing me or watching me, without the water pressure or temperature changing according to how many other people are showering or flushing toilets at the same time. I let my body slip down into the warm water that fills the tub, and I exhale deeply, letting the weight of detention begin to leave my body. At the same time, I can't enjoy the experience completely. I find myself thinking of the other women who are still at Eloy, still separated from their children.

I get out of the bathtub and dry myself off with a thick towel, as white and soft as a cloud. My senses are heightened; everything, even the most mundane object, feels new and almost wondrous. I appreciate things I might have taken for granted before or things I simply never noticed. Though it came as the result of a harsh experience I would never wish upon anyone, I also don't want this new feeling of awareness and gratitude to dissipate. I want to use it to remember the other detained women and their families. Somehow, I want to help them get free, too.

I put on my new clothes and shoes, and tie up the laces. Now, though I carry the scars of trauma inside me, on the outside, I look like any other woman going about her business and her life. I pick up my hotel room key and head to the lobby to meet everyone for dinner. Angeles, the activist wife of a local immigration lawyer, takes us to eat at her father's seafood restaurant.

I think about Lucrecia and the mothers in my Eloy prayer circle as we eat our wonderful meal of succulent shrimp. How much I have wanted to eat something delicious, for so long! But I wish all the mothers were here with us, feeling this immense sense of relief. I think about them again after dinner, as I sink into the comfortable hotel bed, an utter contrast to the metal bunk bed and its thin, worn-out mattress at Eloy. Will the other mothers be as fortunate as I?

————

The moms whose bonds were paid before mine were all taken to their children in a caravan of volunteer drivers, but Immigrant Families Together, the organization the activist moms have formed, has decided to fly me to New York. There are two reasons why they feel safe doing so. First, José will be with me and can intervene if there are any problems. Second, José told the women that he is determined to get my passport back from the detention center, which means—if we're successful—that I'll have an acceptable ID to fly.

The morning after my release, he and I get back into his rental car and return to Eloy. My stomach clenches at the mere thought of being back there, not even twenty-four hours after my release, but José is insistent. I sit in the detention center's waiting room for more than an hour as officials look for my passport. The minutes tick by in torturous slowness. Through a window, I see women shuffling around in those horrible laceless shoes. I wonder whether any of them are the women with whom I'd spent so many hours in conversation and prayer. The distance between captivity and freedom is so short. I want to cry out but refrain, as other people are sitting in the waiting room, too. Instead, I bend my head and pray, passing the agonizing minutes by asking God to stay with these women and give them comfort and hope.

Finally, an officer appears and calls my name, asking me to sign some papers before returning my passport and Fernando's passport to me.

Later that night, on July 12, 2018, José and I arrive at the Phoenix airport and board our flight for New York, along with a camera crew from a New York TV station. The reporter is the same Spanish-speaking white man who had interviewed me just outside Eloy. He seems kind and genuinely concerned, and in the coming days, he will spend a lot of time with me, creating a four-part show for TV, which I agree to do because I want more people to know about what detained immigrant mothers and their children are experiencing.

It is only my second plane ride ever and I'm nervous, but my anxieties are eclipsed by my desire to see Yordy and Fernando and hold them in my arms after eighty-one days apart from them. The plane can't get to New York fast enough.

————

We land in New York City early on the morning of July 13. I'm tired but wound up tight with excitement and uncertainty. Who is waiting for me? What comes next? How long will it take before I can see my sons? What will I do when I see them? What will we do after that? Where will we stay? I have so many questions, and I don't know who to ask for answers. Getting out of detention was hard, and it happened because of God's mercy and grace. We will have to count on Him for everything else to come, too.

José and I walk out of the terminal and into the summer morning. Two women are holding posters that have *"Bienvenidos*, Rosayra" scrawled on them in a large, happy script. They hug me as if we've been friends forever, introducing themselves: *"Soy* Bonnie." *"Soy* Hannah." *"Estamos felices que estás aquí—* we're happy you're here," they say.

But I . . . I feel so strange. I can't believe that these total strangers are welcoming me at the airport at this early hour and supporting me as if they are my own family. I have never experienced anything like this. But the memory of my biblical dream in Eloy comes back to me. God had made a promise then that is now being fulfilled. The light in these women's eyes is an assurance that everything is going to be okay. Immediately, with that reminder from God, I feel an amazing peace wash over me. I feel that I am in the right place at the right time, and that soon, I will finally be with my boys. Not only that, but I have the sense that these people are going to be with me going forward and that they are going to become our family. There are families who are linked by blood and there are families we choose. I'm so lucky. Now, I have both.

———

New York is a noisy place. I'm looking at Bonnie and Hannah and thinking about God and His miracles when a traffic cop blows his whistle sharply and screams at us, "Load it up! Hurry along! Time to go!" A big car is waiting for us, and we all—Bonnie, Hannah, me, José, and the reporter and videographer who were on the flight with us—take turns crawling up into the car and scrambling into a seat. José introduces Julie, the cofounder of Immigrant Families Together, who is driving, and her husband, Francisco.

"She's the one," he says, "who is responsible for all of this."

I don't know what to say. I just sit quietly in the seat behind her.

11

Reunion

As we head west on the Grand Central Parkway, the skyline of New York City begins to come into view. I see buildings that I've seen only in movies: the Chrysler Building; the Empire State Building, or, as my boys will come to call it, "that building King Kong climbed"; the Freedom Tower; hundreds of other buildings whose names I don't know. Everything is big and tall and imposing. The summer sunlight makes the glass and metal gleam brilliantly. Where will I fit in here?

Julie says we will go get breakfast and talk about next steps, but before we even park, get out of the car, and place an order, her phone and mine are both ringing. It's my boys' caseworker at Cayuga Centers, and she says that we need to get there as soon as possible. It's likely that the boys might be released today. We are all incredulous. The promise of coffee and breakfast dissipates, and Julie turns the car toward Harlem, where my boys await.

We park in a lot at Park Avenue and 134th Street and walk four blocks to Cayuga. My insides are a mess. What will happen in the next hour? In the coming days? How will I rebuild a life with my sons after eighty-one days apart? Once we are together again, where will we live? When can I work? What are our next steps? How will we build a life?

Outside Cayuga, a nondescript brick building, a mass of reporters is held at bay behind a metal police fence. Sweat stains the shirtsleeves of some of the men, while women dab at their makeup before the TV cameras are turned on. They strain, leaning over the fence with their microphones, wondering who we are and how we feel. They ask us questions in Spanish and in English. They have been camped out here, we are told, for hours, sweating in New York's unrelenting July sun. Every few minutes a train rumbles by on a track overhead, drowning out the reporters' buzz, and they look annoyed, as if this place, this moment, is only for them. They are eager to film reunifications and releases; they want to broadcast our pain and our joy to thousands of viewers at home, to Americans who are trying to make sense of the zero-tolerance policy and its effects. We are the human faces of this policy and its story, so they zoom in on us with the biggest camera lenses I have ever seen.

The attention is intense and uncomfortable, but I think about the mothers in Eloy and my obligations to them. People need to know what is happening there. I will talk to them later. For now, I let José guide me.

I go into the building and tell security that I am the mother of two boys inside. I explain that the caseworker has called me and told me to show up—now. The security officer puts me in an elevator and presses the button for the third floor. When the door opens, I take a deep breath and walk into the office. Whatever happens next, I'm sure, is God's will.

————

The next hour is a total blur. Cayuga's nerve center is the third floor, where caseworkers' cubicles are protected behind a locked glass door. The receptionist who determines whether someone can get past that door, and then past her, has an unenviable job. The office is busy, and with all the press attention and the number of people trying to get in and out of the building, she is trying to screen people to determine whether they have a valid reason to be there and, if so, how to keep them all in order. There aren't enough chairs for everyone to sit in while they wait to be reunited with their children, and parents crowd every available space in the room, standing in front of the copy machine or hovering over caseworkers' desks, which makes the staff more annoyed.

A number of other people have entered with me and José. There's Yeni, the first mom for whom Immigrant Families Together posted bond. Her three children are at Cayuga, too, and they are being released to her custody today. We've also been accompanied by some politicians who are concerned about family separation, and by several of the women who work with Immigrant Families Together. The receptionist shoos them all away, though, and says that I am the only person who can be in the room when they bring my boys in. Everyone else is told to wait outside or in a separate room where they can't see or interact with the kids coming in or out of the office.

I am shown into a small room and I sit there, alone, waiting for Yordy and Fernando. It sounds strange, but the few minutes I spend here might be the most difficult of our entire separation. I am conscious of wanting the moment they walk in the door to be special; I want to make it something happy and positive, something that they will remember forever after so much pain. I know that our reunion will mark a "before" and an "after," during which we will begin to try to make sense of everything. But with nothing to give them but hugs, kisses, words, and Fernando's little dinosaur, will it be enough?

The door swings open, and a caseworker enters the room. Yordy and Fernando are behind her. My heart! They look different! Both seem like they've grown taller, both seem more filled out. I wrap them in my arms. I stroke their hair. I hold them out at arm's length and look at them intensely. "I love you," I say. "I love you. I told you we would be together again."

————

An hour later, Yordy, Fernando, and I walk out of Cayuga. José, the politicians, and the women from Immigrant Families Together follow us. I'm carrying a thick manila envelope that bulges with the boys' paperwork, and they each have a duffle bag full of clothes. Yordy, who has become a fan of the local baseball team, wears a Yankees cap. The reporters are still there, and now that they see me with the boys, they can hardly contain themselves. They extend their microphones as far as they can reach over the police barricades, and they all shout questions simultaneously.

José steps in front of the cameras and microphones and says some words in English. Then, he invites me to share a few words, a tiny part of our story. I tell the reporters that I am grateful, overwhelmed, and happy—and, also, that I am thinking of all the women I left behind, who have not yet been reunited with their children. I know that those mothers who are still in Eloy can't hear me; they will never see this interview on television. And yet, I hope they know that they have not been forgotten. I will always care for them and carry their stories with me.

It seems like the reporters could go on forever, but the press conference finally comes to an end. As we walk back to the parking lot, I notice that a young, handsome man walking a few paces in front of us keeps turning around and smiling. "That's one of our teachers," Yordy says. The man's smile is so genuine, so tender. He walks a few steps more and turns around again, and repeats the action for two more blocks. Finally, at the next corner, he turns around a final time. He is going left and we are going straight. He crosses his arms, placing his hands together on top of his heart.

"Love," he mouths. "Nothing but love."

PART

II

12

A Wild Idea

Rosayra Pablo Cruz.

Such a beautiful name, I think to myself, though I barely have time to think at all these days. Since June 25, 2018, my life has changed completely. My phone rings with calls and buzzes with text and WhatsApp messages twenty-four hours a day. As soon as I empty my voicemail, it fills up again.

Before June 25, I was a writer, editor, and translator, kept busy by my work and my three children, ages eight, four, and three. But now, I've found myself on the other side of the news cycle, not as a journalist, but as a subject of reporting. Outraged by the family separation policy implemented by the Trump Administration at the Mexico-US border, I have suddenly become a successful fundraiser and activist who is leading a grassroots group that has quickly coalesced into an organization, which we call Immigrant Families Together (IFT), and a movement—one that is confronting me with tough questions about what I want to be doing with my own life.

My most frequent caller is José Orochena. I first heard his name a few days before June 25 in an interview with a reporter on New York's public radio station. I had dropped my husband, Francisco, off at the hospital for an appointment and planned to head back home with our youngest daughter. My phone lit up with a Twitter notification: a group of mothers, many of them with babies strapped to their chests or backs, was occupying the immigration office downtown, a protest intended to express their outrage about the zero-tolerance policy that was separating parents from their children at the Mexico-US border.

"Let's go!" I said to our three-year-old. By the time we got to the immigration office, however, the protest had disbanded so we got back in the car to go home. I was tempted to change the station and listen to some music; lately, the news had become increasingly heavy, almost unbearable. As a mom, as someone who had spent long stretches of time living and traveling in Latin America, and as the wife of a refugee, the images and stories of family separation being filed by journalists in the borderlands carried a particular weight that I couldn't shake.

But I was hoping we might hear something about the protest on the midday news, so I left the station on. Reporter Beth Fertig was speaking with José Orochena, a New York City attorney, who was talking about his client, Yeni, a mother who was in detention in Arizona and whose three children were in New York City's Cayuga Centers. "I think that the only possibility of reuniting Yeni Gonzalez Garcia with her three children is she gets bonded out, comes to New York, and picks up her children and fights her asylum case," he explained. As soon as he said this, I knew, finally, how to answer the unanswered question that had been nagging me for days—"What can I do?"—the same question so many Americans had been asking themselves and each other since we'd learned of the forcible separations that were occurring at the border.

————

I mulled my plan over all afternoon as I got my family ready to attend a silent vigil at Cayuga Centers, where participants piled up children's shoes and stuffed animals in front of the center as a form of protest. I decided to share the plan with Francisco after our kids went to bed.

"I've got this wild idea," I said, as we finished cleaning the kitchen and lined our kids' backpacks up near the door to simplify the next morning's school prep. Sixteen years together have made us finely attuned to each other's strengths and weaknesses, and attuned, too, to the signal phrases that we use to introduce an idea that the other might not necessarily like.

"So, I heard this interview on WNYC today," I began, easing into the conversation. "And it was really interesting. This attorney, a guy named José who's here in the city, says he has this client who's in detention in Arizona. Her kids are here, at Cayuga, the same place where we went to that protest vigil tonight. And then he said something that totally struck me, and I got this wild idea . . ."

"Uh oh," Francisco said, laughing. "I always have to brace

myself when you say that. My mother always warned me how susceptible I am to your 'wild ideas.'"

"Listen," I said, plowing ahead. "So, what he said was this: the mom could come here and reunite with her kids and go through her asylum proceedings in New York—she doesn't have to stay in detention! She only has to do two things: get the bond money and get here."

"Aaaaand?" Francisco asked.

"Well," I said, taking a deep breath, "of course, she can't do either of those things on her own. But I think we could get her out. Let's raise the money and get her here. We have enough friends who are angry about this policy; we're a critical mass! Let's give them a way to do something concrete with their anger! Let's invite them to put their money where their mouths are!"

He dropped the dishcloth in the sink, sat down at the table, and looked at me quietly for a few moments. Thirty-eight years earlier, on an afternoon in late May, he had stepped onto an overloaded boat, the *Green Girl*, bound for the United States, or *La Yuma*. The *Green Girl* was one of hundreds of boats motoring up to the docks in the Cuban port of Mariel that day, one of the thousands that would ferry a mass exodus of Cubans, who would come to be known as Marielitos, out of Mariel between mid-April and late October of 1980.

That day, May 23, he watched as the coast of his island receded, as the boat's motor struggled to propel its load forward, into the deeper waters of the Florida Straits. His chance to leave arose unexpectedly and he made his choice quickly, telling his mother, "I have to leave, now," and making the awful choice to leave behind his nine-month-old son and his son's mother, who didn't want to make the journey. I imagined this was all washing over him now—a tsunami wave of painful memories—as he contemplated my wild idea.

The Mariel boatlift, as that period of migration history came to be called, was prompted by an economic crisis in Cuba. As desperate Cubans sought a solution, ten thousand of them descended upon the Peruvian Embassy in Havana seeking asylum. Fidel Castro, Cuba's president, announced that whoever wanted to defect could do so. The *gusanos*, or worms, as they were named, would be viewed by Castro and his government as traitors in Castro's revolutionary experiment, and they'd be helped out of Cuba by Cuban Americans who had defected a generation earlier after Castro came to power. The Cuban Americans negotiated with US President Jimmy Carter, who agreed to take the *gusanos* in. In the months that ensued, nearly 125,000 Cubans, including the one who would eventually become my husband, landed on the shores of the United States.

Sitting in a boat for ninety miles under a blazing sun beating down on open water leaves you dehydrated and delirious. Francisco was crowded into a boat that was way over capacity, and fear gripped his mind as he and his fellow passengers fought for their own bit of space and breathing room. And there were losses. He has talked about them with me only a handful of times in all these years that we have been together—recounting the horror stories of people who fell overboard, people who could not be saved. Refugee boat captains are like immigrant truck drivers. They just keep moving forward.

―――――――

When he landed in Key West, Francisco was classified as a refugee and was eventually released by immigration into the care of a sponsor, a well-to-do family in Cambridge, Massachusetts—an odd stroke of luck no one has ever been able to explain. They took him in, sheltering and feeding him, until he was able to get on his feet. He was particularly fortunate because so many Marielitos ended up at ad hoc processing centers that looked a lot like the tent cities that are now being used to hold the unaccompanied minors arriving from Central America. Army green tents were set up on military bases and decommissioned missile practice sites, and even on the football field in Florida where the Orange Bowl is held. Once football season started, the tents were moved off the field to underneath an interstate overpass, in vile conditions that one Marielito described as "life in an acoustic torture chamber."

A considerable number of the Marielitos were held for months as the US government tried to figure out how to deal with them. Then it was revealed that Castro had sent a large contingent of Cubans who had been released from prisons and mental institutions along with the exodus of Marielitos.

It was a story Francisco had told me a hundred times, and each time I heard it, I felt immense gratitude for the family who took him in. Tales from that chapter in his life have worked their way into our shared family lore, like the one about the time the family asked him how Cubans say "cake."

"Cake," he said, "we say cake."

"No, no, no," they said. "How do YOU say 'cake'?," refusing to believe that Cubans use the same word for "cake" as Americans. Now, every time we have cake, we say, "No, no, no, how do YOU say 'cake'?"

He lost contact with that family years ago, but I have often fantasized about finding them, about letting them know he's turned out all right—no doubt largely thanks to them. I have dreamed about telling them what he has done with his life, about his children, about what an incredible father and partner he is, and about what he still dreams of doing.

He was probably thinking of them, too, as we sat in silence. "I want to call José Orochena on Monday and tell him my plan, see whether he's interested," I finally said. "But before I do that, I need to know: Are you in? Because this is a commitment, and once we make it, we can't back out."

"I'm in," he said. "How could I not be?"

———

That weekend, Francisco, our kids, and some friends and I hosted a donations drive for the New York–area foster-care centers that were taking in children who had been separated from their parents at the border. It was an event we had already planned before I'd heard the radio interview with José, and we watched in awe as our friend Maria's living room filled with donations—everything you could imagine kids would want and need: toys and stuffed animals, books and crayons, clothing and shoes, diapers and wipes, and so much more, even baby bathtubs and strollers and car seats. Within a couple of hours, we couldn't walk comfortably through the living room, and someone had to clear a path so we could get to the kitchen and the bathroom.

We had announced the drive on Facebook, sharing the request for donations mainly among friends. But somehow, even moms from New Jersey had heard about the event, and they loaded up two cars packed full of brand-new items and drove in from the suburbs. Our kids sold agua fresca and lemonade on the sidewalk. They told passersby that their proceeds were going to help families who were separated at the border, and soon, they were accepting $10 and $20 donations from people who didn't even want a drink. "Keep the money," they said. "You're doing good work."

Meanwhile, as the adults sorted the donated goods into piles, I called U-Haul to reserve a truck so we could move everything once it was repacked. The kids raised enough money to pay for the truck, and we filled it up. A group of us caravanned in the U-Haul and our cars to take the delivery to Riverside Church, where more volunteers would sort the items again and designate them for specific foster-care centers. As I looked at the church's spire jutting high into the blue sky, I couldn't help but think of the generations of activists who came to this sacred space before us, including, especially, Dr. Martin Luther King Jr., who offered his stirring "Beyond Vietnam" speech here in 1967.

I thought of at least a dozen lines from that discourse that applied to those of us moving the items out of the truck and into the church. I took a moment to step into the vast sanctuary with its soaring, vaulted ceiling. I gazed at the pulpit, wishing I had been present when Dr. King intoned: "Some of us who have already begun to break the silence of the night have found that the calling to speak is often a vocation of agony, but we must speak. . . . For we are deeply in need of a new way beyond the darkness that seems so close around us." And he continued, "A true revolution of values will soon cause us to question the fairness and justice of many of our past and present policies." I could imagine the straightening of his back and the strengthening of his voice as he built up toward his stirring conclusion with the words: "Over the bleached bones and jumbled residues of numerous civilizations are written the pathetic words, 'Too late.' There is an invisible book of life that faithfully records our vigilance or our neglect."

I stepped out of the sanctuary and back into the lobby, where people were moving to and fro like a line of hardworking ants, working in collaboration with one another, each with their own role. When we dropped off our donations, the room where church volunteers were receiving items was already packed wall-to-wall and floor-to-ceiling with similar items. Cars, trucks, and vans were double- and triple-parked in front of the church, creating a bonanza for traffic cops, as donors and volunteers alike formed lined brigades to move donations into the church. Inside, still more volunteers prepped boxes and bags and moved them back out to the sidewalk, where they were picked up by drivers who would deliver them to the foster-care centers.

The response to our donations drive and the sheer volume of volunteers coming and going at Riverside Church made me more confident in my idea than anything I'd ever attempted in my whole life. Clearly, family separation was a galvanizing issue, and people wanted to get involved, doing anything they could to express their dissent and to extend comfort to the families who were affected by the zero-tolerance policy. The groundswell of support convinced me. I was certain that we could raise enough money to get Yeni González García out of detention in Arizona and reunite her with her children in New York.

On Monday, June 25, I woke up and Googled José Orochena. It turned out he was a DUI attorney, not an immigration attorney, though he'd already begun his crash course in the specialty. He'd been roped into the family separation fracas by Yeni's family in North Carolina. Upon learning that their nephews and niece were separated from Yeni at the border, they sprang into action, searching on the internet for a Spanish-speaking attorney near Cayuga Centers. José was the first result that popped up.

I called him and was surprised that he picked up on the first ring. "Hi, my name is Julie Schwietert Collazo, and I heard you on WNYC last week talking about your client, the one in Arizona." I shared my wild idea with José and concluded by asking, "Would this be of interest to you and your client?"

He laughed. "Would it be of interest to me and my client?" he repeated, still laughing. "OF COURSE it would be of interest to us! This is what we needed!" He explained that Yeni's family might be able to raise part of the bond money, but certainly not all of it, though even he didn't know yet how much her bond would be. I told him I wanted to go ahead and start fundraising if it was okay with him.

I ended the conversation by explaining that I was a former social worker, and so I wanted to assure him and his client that this was not some do-gooder project intended to make myself or donors feel like we deserved a medal or a pat on the back. I told him we were in this for the long haul and that we wouldn't just pay the bond, get her to New York, and say, "Goodbye, and good luck." No. We understood, even at that early juncture, that in order for this family to have a fighting chance, we would have to provide ongoing support, financial and otherwise—that we would have to become and embody the idea of the "beloved community," as articulated by Dr. King. José thanked me for my call and said he'd be in touch as soon as he knew the bond amount.

That night, I launched the first GoFundMe campaign, calling it Team Yeni. I posted about it on Facebook, setting the status to "public." The following morning, José called to say that Yeni's bond was set at $7,500. Within twenty-four hours, we had raised that amount—and more. Much more. Donations kept rolling in. Within just two days, more than 250 people had contributed a total of $17,347, and there was no indication that donations would slow down anytime soon. As people who were heartbroken about family separation kept supporting the GoFundMe campaign and telling other people about it on social media, I did two things: I called José to say we were ready to post Yeni's bond; and then, I started marshaling the volunteers who had materialized out of the blue, listening to what they had to offer and putting them to work.

———

Sara Farrington, one of the New Jersey moms who had driven a load of donations to Queens, was eager to take her volunteerism a step farther. She felt good about the items she had collected, but she wanted to do more, much more. A cadre of moms in her community were ready to host any mother who needed housing, she said. But perhaps more important, Sara, who worked for a mega-corporation by day and wrote plays by night while caring for her own two young children, had a network of friends in the theater world whom she thought could be helpful.

One of them was Meghan Finn, producer and co–artistic director of the Off-Broadway performance venue The Tank. Meghan, who had just taken this position, her dream job, a year earlier, managed to keep the theater running smoothly while also playing the vital role of what we would come to call the "Control Tower." In a matter of mere hours, she mapped out a route for Yeni's road trip across the United States, identified trustworthy drivers and hosts, and coordinated a complex journey with limited—okay, no—resources. Like Sara, she was a mom of two young boys. She quickly became our most essential volunteer, holding down her demanding full-time job and being an amazing, attentive mother to her own kids, while logging late nights coordinating IFT operations.

José was astonished. It wasn't just that we had raised Yeni's bond so quickly. It was also that we had what seemed to be an incredibly well-coordinated plan to get her safely across the country and back to her children. "You're some crazy, badass ladies!" he told us admiringly. At the time, he didn't know just how crazy, badass, or capable we really were.

Neither did we.

———

José and I nurtured our working relationship via text. The DUI-attorney-turned-immigration-crusader was the father of young children, and the calls from the detention center touched a parental nerve. A solo practitioner, he was taking on more and more cases, most of them pro bono. He knew that it probably wasn't a smart business move, but he took on as many cases as he could and racked up some frequent flyer miles shuttling between New York and Phoenix.

I paid Yeni's bond on June 28, and she was released later that day. Control Tower Finn alerted the caravan of drivers, monitoring Yeni's progress every mile of the trip and keeping our growing core team of volunteers apprised of her estimated arrival in New York City. Along the way, Yeni met the best of the United

States. Her drivers included volunteers in the sanctuary movement, a rabbi and father who was deeply disturbed by the family separation policy, and an immigrant dad, among others. They put their own lives on hold and drove through the day, each leg of the journey bringing her miles closer to her children.

At night, more volunteers welcomed Yeni into their homes, feeding her and offering hospitality that they hoped would play a small part in healing the harm that Trump Administration policies had done to her and her children. Some of them looked up Guatemalan recipes online and cooked meals they hoped would comfort her. Her stomach was struggling to take in food after detention, but she appreciated their thoughtfulness. Most of the volunteers spoke no Spanish, but they did their best, communicating via Google Translate.

Videographers from *TIME* rode along for much of the journey, and by the time Yeni reached Newark, New Jersey, media coverage was intensifying. A reporter and photographer from the *New York Times* joined Yeni in the car after Senator Cory Booker helped her to move her luggage from one car to another for the last leg of her trip.

Meanwhile, in New York City, excitement was building, with two groups of supporters waiting to welcome her. One waited on the south side of Central Park, and among them was the then–public advocate Letitia James, who would go on to become New York State's attorney general. The other welcome group waited at Courthouse Square in Long Island City, a neighborhood in Queens, which has been called the most culturally diverse county in the United States. That fact was certainly reflected in the identities of those who gathered in anticipation of Yeni's arrival. In addition to ordinary citizens who had shown up, there was a senator and an assemblywoman and other elected officials, as well as candidates running for elected office. All denounced the zero-tolerance policy; some even called to abolish ICE. Well-wishers carried signs of welcome in various languages. Some brought flowers. A Muslim woman came bearing a bracelet that she would put on Yeni's wrist. It read, "She thought she could, so she did."

Around 6:30 p.m., Yeni's car pulled up in front of the courthouse. The crowd broke into applause and cheers. Meghan Finn and the core team of volunteers convened on WhatsApp and released a collective sigh of relief and celebration. We'd done it. With the help of thousands of donors and a dozen drivers and hosts, we had freed Yeni from detention and brought her safely across the country—more than twenty-four hundred miles—to reunite with her children.

———

Posting Yeni's bond and getting her to New York attracted an absurd amount of press coverage in the process. Telemundo, TalkPoverty, WNYC, *TIME*, the *New York Times*, CNN . . . the list went on and on. It wouldn't be long before I realized that perhaps Yeni had been overexposed, but she and José had assured me that she wanted to continue speaking to the media; she wanted to make sure that the mothers who remained at Eloy, and other detention centers, weren't forgotten. She wanted to ensure that public sentiment would be encouraged to support their release and facilitate their reunification with their children.

The press, of course, generated more donations, and people often made their contributions with notes appended, indicating that they'd heard about us on the *Rachel Maddow Show* or NY1, that they'd read about us in *USA Today* or *Teen Vogue*. Thousands of people watched a video about Yeni on the website NowThis. The video was filmed by a seventy-four-year-old freelance journalist named Sandi Bachom, who had done work about Holocaust survivors and had covered (and been injured during) the white supremacist rally in Charlottesville, Virginia, a year earlier. Sandi knew how to convey the essence of the story of the crises provoked by family separation, and the video quickly went viral, generating hundreds of donations and messages from well-wishers, many of whom asked us to express to Yeni and her family that they were sorry for what the United States had done to them.

As Yeni reunited with her children and settled into her life in New York, José was fielding an increasing number of calls from Eloy. He had a growing list of names, mothers who were also separated from their children under the zero-tolerance policy. Aware of Yeni's release, they had contacted him in desperation, wondering whether he could help them, too. Though it might have been to the detriment of his practice and his financial well-being, he couldn't say no. In turn, he contacted me and said,

"You're public enemy number one at Eloy because you've given women hope."

And then he asked, "Can you do it again?"

————

The day after Yeni arrived in New York, José came to my home for a strategy meeting with IFT's central team, a group that had coalesced rapidly, even as it was building an extended network of volunteers across the country, with a particularly strong cohort in California. All of us were parents with full-time jobs and other responsibilities, but like José, the family separation policy shook us to our cores and we couldn't turn away. We were meeting because José had more detained mothers with bond offers he wanted us to consider, and we wanted to plan the next few days' worth of work.

As we sat around my kitchen table, José presented us with a list of names, bond amounts, and locations where mothers needed to go upon release to be reunited with their children. How many of them could we free and help reunite with their families? As we discussed the details of the mothers who had contacted him and asked for help, José's phone rang. "This is a call from Eloy Detention Center," an automated voice said. "Press '1' to accept this call, '2' to decline." José, of course, pressed "1." He took the name and information of the mother on the line and added her to our burgeoning roster. He told her to be strong, that we'd do whatever we could to get her free and back with her children. She wept and said she hoped God would bless him for what he was doing. The call disconnected and José rubbed his tired eyes before bidding us good night. He hadn't seen much of his own children lately, and he wanted to get home so he could tuck them in.

———

After José left, the core team discussed Yeni's arrival: what we had done well, what we had learned, and what, in retrospect, we wished we had done differently. For one thing, we acknowledged, we wanted to be more deliberate in our collaboration with the media. We hadn't expected quite so much press attention, and it was clear that the avalanche of interview requests and press conferences had been stressful for Yeni, even as she reaffirmed that she wanted to speak to the media in order to bring attention to the family separation policy and what was happening in Eloy.

In addition to the family separation policy, she was keen to draw attention to the conditions inside the detention center, conditions that, increasingly, we suspected, were not isolated to Eloy. Yeni's cell mate, Irma, was a mother for whom we would post bond within weeks. In detention, Yeni confirmed, Irma had been seriously ill. She couldn't hold food down—in fact, she found it difficult to eat at all—and she was vomiting blood. Irma had gone to the sick bay a number of times, Yeni said, describing her symptoms to officials, but each time she was sent back to her cell with the same useless advice: drink more water and take ibuprofen. Yeni recalled that Irma looked sick and that her condition worsened over the period of their detention, but officials never seemed willing to intervene.

When Irma was released on July 17, 2018, she reunited with her two children, who had been released from foster care and into the custody of her sister, who lived in California. Within days, Irma showed up at the local hospital's emergency room. Her symptoms were severe, even more acute than they had been at Eloy; now, she couldn't eat anything at all. The diagnosis was even worse than we all feared: Irma had rapidly advancing cancer of the esophagus. Doctors predicted that she had five years, at most, to live.

One doctor would ultimately opine that ICE had neglected to diagnose and treat Irma, whose symptoms outpaced the doctors' prognosis. After a brief but vicious battle with the aggressive cancer, she passed away at her home in California on September 7, 2019. As per her wishes, her body was sent back to Guatemala for burial.

―――――

At the time, one of the requirements for parents who wanted to regain custody of their children was to prove that they had income. It was a ridiculous criterion, a Catch-22 dilemma, as parents were not allowed to work. Francisco and I went into a meeting at Cayuga Centers with a printout showing how much money we had raised for Yeni via GoFundMe.

"Would $30,000 be enough income?" I asked the director of social services and the agency's lead counsel. The social services director said she thought $30,000 would be fine, admitting that they didn't really know whether there was even a threshold number that parents had to meet to prove that their income was adequate. "The policy seems to change each day," she said in a tired voice. "We come into work each day and there are new directives. We're just trying to keep up."

————

On the afternoon of July 3, our core team had a planning phone call. During the call, Meghan Finn threw an ambitious idea out on the table: Why not leverage the occasion of Independence Day to raise an absurd amount of money within twenty-four hours? How much money, exactly, I asked? Forty thousand dollars, she said, which would allow us to post bond for multiple moms. Independence indeed!

I gulped. This was growing bigger by the day and it made me a bit anxious, but we had nothing to lose by trying. Within an hour, another volunteer had the GoFundMe pages up for the new bonds that José had passed along to us, and we started promoting the Independence Day campaign.

I was as astonished as anyone to see that we raised $30,000 of our goal within just twelve hours. Even my own father, a lifelong Republican and former member of the National Rifle Association, donated a large sum of money to our cause. There were other surprises, too. Conservative friends and acquaintances, I noticed, had shared the GoFundMe links. The outrage and disgust around the Trump Administration's zero-tolerance policy and the practice of family separation clearly crossed party lines. Even people who considered themselves uninterested in or unaffected by immigration issues and policies were horrified by the images of children in cages and asylum seekers huddled under thin Mylar blankets. A line had been crossed, and an inviolable one. You could be opposed to immigration but still feel in your core that something was inarguably, morally wrong about separating parents from their children, particularly in such a disorganized and inhumane way.

As reports circulated about the conditions under which parents and children were separated, and the conditions in which they were being held, some people raised the questions: Were we headed toward a twenty-first-century version of the Holocaust? And if we failed to act swiftly and denounce what was happening, would we be complicit? Online comments that people submitted along with their donations seemed to suggest that they believed the answers to both questions were a resounding yes.

The Independence Day fundraiser was so successful that it allowed us to post bond for our second and third moms, Juana and Amalia, who had been detained at Eloy. Now, they were free and headed to reunite with their children and families. Control Tower Finn managed two teams of volunteer drivers who traced two distinct routes, one heading north to New York and the other heading south to Florida. In New York, TV crews from CNN en Español and the PBS series *Frontline* were waiting for Juana, and their coverage of her story drew even more urgent attention to the zero-tolerance policy and its harmful effects. In Florida, volunteers were already organized to provide Amalia with full-scale support, including connecting her with legal counsel and social service providers who could assist with other needs. (Amalia and her two sons became the first family supported by IFT to be granted legal asylum in the United States, in April 2019.)

What had we created? We weren't a formal group, and we didn't particularly have a strategy. What might we be able to do if we *really* organized? I was both excited and terrified by the possibilities. A former social worker, I'd left the nonprofit world fifteen years earlier, disillusioned by its limitations, especially its unnecessary bureaucracy and waste, and the fact that skilled social workers were rarely allowed to do their best work because of these obstacles. Returning to the world of social service to confront those dilemmas anew wasn't particularly appealing to me. Plus, I wasn't looking for a new job. I had plenty of satisfying work. Not to mention, I had my own three kids to raise. Did I *really* want to continue scaling this grassroots effort, as a number of people and potential funders were already encouraging me to do?

There was no time to ponder those questions deeply, however, and Meghan had no time to recover from her round-the-clock task because on July 11, we were planning to post bond for three more mothers: Floridalma, Lilian, and Rosayra, each of whom would be headed to a different state.

In Spanish, there's a saying I've always loved: *Aprendí caminando*, I learned by walking. That described IFT pretty well. We were learning as we went along, learning just by doing the work. The money kept coming in, and we kept posting bond, reuniting moms with their children, and building structures of support around them so that they could have the greatest chance possible of building a safe and stable life with their families while they pursued their asylum claims, regardless of the outcome rendered by an immigration judge.

———

I first learned of Rosayra in a text message from José, which he sent to me on the morning of July 9. The message included three photos. Each photo was a records page from ICE's "Online Detainee Locator" website, and each page contained the name of a woman, her country of birth, her alien number, and the name of the detention facility where she was currently in custody. Each page also had additional notes scribbled by José, such as where the woman's children were in foster care, whether she had other family in the United States, contact information for any family members, and details about how and when the mothers had been separated from their children.

One additional handwritten notation on each records page stood out because it had been marked with an orange highlighter: the amount of each mother's bond. Lilian's bond was set at $25,000. It was the most expensive bond we had seen yet. Floridalma's bond was $10,000, and Rosayra's was $12,000.

"Any chance that we can get them bonded out Thursday?" José wrote. He was headed back to Arizona and wanted to be present when the three mothers were released. He had quickly gotten media savvy and was as open to press requests as he was to the pleas of mothers to represent him. In New York, he had negotiated appearances with Yeni on CNN's *Cuomo Prime Time*, among other outlets. In Arizona, he had organized his own press conference outside Eloy, and he wanted to take advantage of the multiple releases to really push the family separation agenda in the news.

"Yes," I told him, "we can post bond Thursday, if not sooner." I headed to the bank to have three cashier's checks cut, one for each mother's bond. *Forty-seven thousand dollars*, I thought to myself. *This is what the US government has decided these three lives are worth.*

As the bank teller pulled the checks from the printer, I told her that she had just played a small but important role in ensuring that three mothers who were separated from their children at the border would be freed and reunited with them. She covered her mouth with her hand and then smiled. "I did?" she asked, adding that she had been watching the news about this issue closely. She was perplexed and angry about such a cruel policy, she said, and she asked me to wish the mothers well.

I stuffed the $47,000 worth of checks deep in my bag. I had never been responsible for so much money in my life, and I kept looking over my shoulder as I walked south on Broadway toward 26 Federal Plaza, the building where New York City's immigration field office, immigration courts, and bond office are all housed. Did anyone know I had thousands of dollars in my bag? I knew they didn't, but I still felt like a marked woman. A strong wind blew down Broadway, and though the checks were tucked safely underneath the books and laptop I carried in my bag, I was worried they could blow away, swirling all the way to the Hudson River where it empties into the Atlantic Ocean, right at the feet of the Statue of Liberty.

Just a few days earlier, on the same day we were raising the money for these bonds, an activist named Patricia Okoumou had climbed Lady Liberty in protest of the family separation policy. Her action drew massive attention, and I thought to myself, *This is what it's going to take: a critical mass of us willing to do both little and big things to push back against zero tolerance.* I felt a kinship with Okoumou, and with the growing number of activists I was meeting through my work with IFT. With each day that passed, I found that my desire to focus on my editing work was waning. I sat in on conference calls listening to clients talk about their corporate blogs and communication strategies, and I wanted to interrupt them to say, "Don't you know what's happening to families on the border? No one cares how many times a week you post on your corporate blog!" My waking hours—and there weren't many sleeping ones—were increasingly being consumed by the work of reuniting separated families.

———

I made it to 26 Federal Plaza and was waved through security, an airport-style checkpoint with x-ray machines for bags, metal detectors for bodies, and agents who are always on edge, expecting the worst of their fellow humans. Inside, I noticed the smiling, self-assured faces of President Trump and Vice President Pence beaming down from portraits hung at least ten feet high on the wall. The lobby of the building was abuzz with activity, as asylum seekers, refugees, and immigrants about to be sworn in as US citizens in the weekly naturalization ceremony consulted the building directory to see which floor and which room attended to their particular need. To one side of the lobby, women had set up several tables and were selling jewelry and purses, all from other countries, their sign boasted.

I headed to the main bank of elevators and pressed the button for the ninth floor. When the doors opened, I walked into the bond office and requested three forms. "Three?" the agent replied, arching an eyebrow. "Yes, three," I confirmed. He pushed the forms through the slot in the window that divided him and his colleagues from the waiting room.

I took a clipboard and a pen and sat down to fill out the forms. The pen, a basic ballpoint, was affixed to a yellow plastic spoon with electrical tape. I listed each woman's name, country of origin, and the address where she would be living after her release, as well as my own information as the obligor, or the person who pays the bond.

In my July 9 text messages with José, he hadn't just passed along the basic information I needed about each woman in order to fill out the bond forms. We also messaged back and forth about where each woman was going and with whom she was going to live. Floridalma would be heading to southern Georgia, where her husband awaited her with their children, who had been released to him after they had been taken from Floridalma at the border.

Why such a small, Deep South town? I wondered. I had lived in Georgia during college and had never heard of the town where Floridalma would be living. A cursory Google search proved it wasn't an immigrant-friendly place, but there was work, and that was probably the reason Floridalma's family lived there. A chicken-processing plant attracted immigrants, both documented and undocumented, who performed the largely invisible labor that US-born Americans don't want to do—the labor that keeps food on our tables and keeps the country running. After reading about the frequency of ICE raids in the town, I made a mental note to see whether the family wanted to move to a larger city where, I thought, they could be closer to services and support and get jobs where they were less likely to be swept back up into the detention machine via an unexpected ICE raid.

Lilian would have a shorter trip. Her first stop would be Texas, where her son Wanner was still in foster care in the custody of Lutheran Social Services in Corpus Christi. With the aid of a lawyer and two volunteers, she would eventually regain custody and settle near Houston. Her attorney, Mana Yegani, would become an essential legal defender in the fight against zero tolerance, representing another family supported by our group and even paying for their medicine and taking them Christmas presents when she realized they had no local support—and no heat in their chilly apartment.

Of the three women for whom we were posting bond that day, though, Rosayra was of the greatest concern to me. Though she had initially planned to return to Chicago, where she had lived during her previous time in the United States, the person with whom she thought she and her boys would be able to live decided that they couldn't take the family in after all. We would see this scenario play out again and again in the coming months, as ICE targeted sponsors and family members of people who were detained in an effort to see whether they could round up undocumented folks. Spooked, the people who had promised to help mothers and their children settle into life in the United States would suddenly revoke their offer of support, leaving families without a Plan B and scrambling to figure out how to move forward.

When the obligor fills out the bond paperwork, he or she is required to indicate where the detained person is going to live upon release. Officers take that address and use Google Street View and other real estate websites to confirm that the location is legitimate. Rosayra didn't have an address, and ICE wouldn't release her without one. José told me to use his office and his phone number as her future contact information. I wrote his address on the form and then submitted it to the officer for review. He asked for my ID and the bond checks, and made a photocopy of each, stapling them to the bond forms.

I sat in the stuffy waiting room, which is papered with signs that make liberal use of capitalized, bold, and italicized letters, and frequent use of the word "NO":

PAYING A BOND IS A LONG PROCESS.
NO BONDS WILL BE EXCEPTED [*sic*] AFTER 3 PM
NO EXCEPTIONS.

BOND POLICY: FOR BONDS $10,000 AND OVER—
ONE (1) CERTIFIED CASHIER'S CHECK;
FOR BONDS UNDER $10,000—MONEY ORDERS
(LIMIT OF 10 ARE ACCEPTED) US POSTAL SERVICE
NO EXCEPTIONS
**NO CELL PHONES. NO FOOD. NO DRINKS.
NO EXCEPTIONS**

I began to realize the enormousness of what we had taken on. My initial plan, the "wild idea" I had presented to my husband on June 21, was to raise the money and post bond for *one* mother and get her to New York City to reunite with her children. Suddenly, in a matter of just a couple of weeks, we had raised enough money to free multiple mothers and we were sketching out support plans for their post-release lives. How had this scaled so much and so quickly? The days since late June—not even a month!—had passed in a total blur.

Though I had been a social worker, a profession whose knowledge base, skills, and contacts were certainly coming in handy, the family separation situation and all that it had wrought presented me with a massive learning curve, and I soon discovered that this was the case even for individuals and organizations that had far more experience than IFT volunteers did. In fact, administrators from other respected organizations with much longer histories and greater resources were calling me and asking, "How have you managed to do this? Why are you so fast and so effective?"

The simple answer was that we were harnessing people's outrage and desperation about the cruelty of family separation and giving them a way to channel those feelings into doing something concretely useful. As it turned out, a group of angry moms who were adept at using social media could raise massive amounts of money, and then, because we weren't a formal organization with bylaws and boards of directors, we could make decisions and take actions with a speed that's uncharacteristic of—and impossible for—most nonprofits.

We were also skilled at telling the stories of the moms and their families and explaining how donations were supporting them. This part was key. The stories let donors know that their money—every single penny—was going directly to the families we were supporting. With no office, no salaries, and no operational costs, we could make a dollar go a very long way, even in the face of inflated bond amounts, which were becoming increasingly common. When journalists asked where we were headquartered, I responded, "My living room." And I wasn't joking. They'd show up to confirm this for themselves, annoying my neighbors, some of whom were beginning to complain about the frequent news cameras and TV vans parked outside our building. Others came up to us quietly in the hall or elevator and slipped us money or a gift card for food. "What you're doing is important," they'd whisper. "Keep going."

The IFT volunteers coordinated via WhatsApp from our homes and offices or while picking our kids up from school or playing with them at the park or watching them blow bubbles at a birthday party. We tapped out text messages with one hand while holding a nursing baby with the other. One volunteer, Sara Nolan, wrote thank-you notes to GoFundMe donors while waiting out contractions before going to the hospital in labor. Another, Courtney Sullivan, went to pay a bond on the same day she was due to deliver her second child. We called in favors from old friends and acquaintances—"Hey! I know we haven't talked in a few years, but is there any chance you could host a mom just released from immigration detention at your home in Phoenix tonight?"—and leaned on others for all sorts of assistance. We held near-nightly calls on a free conference call line we found on the internet. We ate cereal for dinner, and so did our kids. Always, in the background, a baby was babbling or a toddler was asking for a snack, and nobody batted an eye about it or complained that it prevented us from getting things done. Most of us were at the same intense juncture in our lives: that phase when multitasking is a given, sleep is elusive, and everything is doable and gets done because there is no other choice.

And most of us were parents. The thought that other mothers were sitting in cells, separated from their children, kept us going.

———

The sign in the immigration office isn't wrong: the bond process *is* long. In the summer of 2018, I spent entire days of my life on the ninth floor of 26 Federal Plaza. Waiting for three bonds to be processed, especially when the detention facility is in another time zone, as Eloy is, makes for a full day at the office.

As I waited for Floridalma's, Lilian's, and Rosayra's bonds to be processed, I texted José. "Do Rosayra and her kids need a place to live?" I asked. "Yes," he answered. With plenty of time to kill before the officers would call my name, sign the bond receipts, and issue copies to me, I turned to my phone and scrolled through my messages and contacts. I needed housing for a mom and two kids . . . in New York City . . . quickly. Who could help?

In addition to the thousands of dollars of donations that had resulted in my inbox being flooded with notifications from Go-FundMe, I was receiving dozens and dozens of messages every day, and via every possible medium, from people who wanted to help in other ways. Americans who were desperate to get involved in our effort somehow found my phone number, filling up my voicemail. They sent text messages and Facebook friend requests or tagged me on Twitter. "How can I help?" they asked. "Money isn't enough. I want to *do* something, anything. Tell me what to do."

Other messages articulated exactly what the person reaching out had to offer: "I can drive from Phoenix to Denver." "I live in Greensboro, North Carolina, and I'm happy to host a mother in my home overnight if we live along one of your routes." "I'm a chef, and I'd like to cook for the families. Tell me how I can help." "I'm a trauma therapist, and I'm available to offer pro bono counseling." I received innumerable offers of extra rooms and extra beds in cities and towns all across the United States.

Some of the messages contained truly astonishing offers: "I am a pilot with a private plane; I'll be happy to fly any families in need of reunification within six hours of New York." No matter how modest or outlandish the offer, a volunteer—one of the few childfree volunteers among us, a twenty-year-old actor named Zoë—logged them *all* on a spreadsheet, further organizing them by geographic location. While we strove to reply to everyone, the volume of messages quickly made that unsustainable. Nevertheless, we kept the spreadsheet up-to-date; we never knew when we might need someone in Cincinnati or Des Moines, in Nashville or Tampa. And hey, maybe we'd actually need that private plane at some point, too.

———

Early on in the existence of Immigrant Families Together, numerous faith groups reached out to us to offer support, too. Synagogues and their rabbis were most prominent in number among them, and those from New York were uniquely poised to extend a hand. Shortly after the announcement of the zero-tolerance policy, they had mobilized to either activate or form refugee task forces or committees, and they had acted quickly to denounce the policy, issuing a joint open letter to then–Attorney General Jeff Sessions, who was viewed as the architect of the policy, and then–Secretary of Homeland Security Kirstjen Nielsen, whose agency was in charge of carrying it out.

In the letter, which was signed by more than 350 Jewish organizations representing Reform, Reconstructionist, Conservative, and Orthodox movements, they warned that "taking children away from their families . . . inflict[s] unnecessary trauma on parents and children, many of whom have already suffered traumatic experiences." The consequences of such cumulative trauma were severe, they cautioned, and could include an increased "risk of early death." They concluded by reflecting upon their own history and spiritual tenets: "Our Jewish faith demands of us concern for the stranger in our midst. Our own people's history as 'strangers' reminds us of the many struggles faced by immigrants today and compels our commitment to an immigration system in this country that is compassionate and just."

Though they didn't make the reference overtly in the open letter, many of the signatories and members of their organizations or synagogues were talking privately among themselves about the alarming parallels they saw between the ways in which the zero-tolerance policy was being carried out and the Holocaust. Increasingly, the media were also drawing such comparisons. The *Los Angeles Times* printed a selection of letters it received from Holocaust survivors who described the long-lasting pain of having been separated from their parents and articulated their worries for the children who were being impacted by zero tolerance. "'Never again' has become an empty promise," wrote Holocaust survivor and author Josie Levy Martin.

One of the signatories of the joint open letter was a Brooklyn synagogue, Beth Elohim. The Reform congregation had deep roots firmly planted in a number of social justice movements, especially those that seek to combat racism and xenophobia and create truly inclusive spaces and communities. Its Refugee Task Force was already involved in the resistance to zero tolerance, and they wanted to do more. They had some concrete ideas about how they could help, but they also came to us with a simple question: "What do you need?"

———

What we needed now, I thought, as the clock ticked into my fourth hour at the bond office, *was a place for Rosayra, Yordy, and Fernando to live*. It needn't be a permanent home, though that would be incredible. Even a temporary home would do, as long as it was safe and clean and, ideally, rent-free. Rabbi Rachel Timoner, who was inspired by the opportunity to take concrete action that would have a big effect on the life of a family, put out the word among the members of her congregation, and I received a call right away. Would a three-story home in Park Slope be suitable? I felt like José must have felt when I called him the first time, and I laughed. That sounded just fine.

The owners of the house were out of town for the summer and would be happy to turn their home over to Rosayra and her sons. They hoped it would be a place where the family could begin to heal from the wounds of being forcibly separated. They could move in as soon as Rosayra arrived in New York and would need to move out at the end of August, when the owners would return. The arrangement was sweetened by the fact that the synagogue was right around the corner, and its congregants, particularly the members of its Refugee Task Force, would volunteer to be the core support team for Rosayra and her sons and would help raise money for their needs, too. The Refugee Task Force members would help Rosayra, Yordy, and Fernando settle in. They would show them the neighborhood, teach them how to navigate the subway system with confidence, and have them over for dinner regularly. Their kids could play soccer with Yordy at a nearby field or run through the sprinkler with Fernando at a local playground. I texted José to let him know that the family was set: they had a perfect, safe temporary place to live and we'd find a longer-term situation later.

As I pressed "Send" on that text, the officer called me to the window and asked me to sign each of the three bond receipts. Floridalma, Lilian, and Rosayra were moving one step closer to their freedom. On each bond worksheet, there's a line where the obligor can write a note to the detained person. "*FUERZA*— Strength," I'd written to each woman, wondering if she'd actually receive the message. I picked up the stylus and touched it to a small digital screen, adding my signature, three times for each receipt. "Sit down until we call your name again," the officer said. The wait now is for the time it takes the officers to print the bond receipts and stamp "ORIGINAL" in blue ink across the first page. Each bond receipt consists of three pages, to which are stapled three more pages that list the terms and conditions of the bond.

My name, my home address, and my Social Security number were all typed onto every bond form. My signature indicated my understanding of and agreement to the terms of being an obligor. Chief among them is this: to declare that I am "firmly bound unto the United States . . . that the alien shall not become a public charge." So far, every one of the moms for whom we'd posted bond and whom I'd met in person or talked to by phone wanted to work and to take on the responsibility of caring for her family and contributing to society in a meaningful way—when she was legally permitted to do so. In the meantime, the work of Immigrant Families Together was to ensure that she had everything she needed so she wouldn't become a public charge—and so she could start to rebuild her life, with her children at her side.

13

Rebuilding a Family

When Rosayra and her boys stepped out of Cayuga Centers and into the sunlight, media cameras turned on their brighter lights. Photographers pushed their lenses over the shoulders of reporters in front of them, and correspondents grabbed microphones and pushed them as far forward in the crowd as they could. Holding Fernando's hand, with the boys' discharge paperwork in manila folders tucked under her other arm, Rosayra stopped in front of the reporters and said, "Thank you, New York." Then, even if she thought they'd never hear her words, she offered remarks directed specifically to other detained mothers. "I call on all mothers not to lose hope. To keep faith. There are good people, people with great big hearts."

Yordy and Fernando stood at her side, holding hands, a bit dazed by the attention that was trained on them, even though they had become accustomed to seeing TV cameras and photographers camped outside the foster-care center. Journalists who wanted to learn more about what was happening inside the facility—which was as well-defended as a fortress, with security guards and police officers—spent days outside Cayuga, trying to take photos of the separated children who were dropped off there each morning by their foster families and then picked up again in the afternoon. At one point, the media had become so intense that Cayuga staff had given the children paper animal masks to cover their faces, directing them to put these on as they entered or exited the facility.

————

Once Rosayra and her boys had moved beyond the camera lights, Yordy seemed to feel free to cry. As volunteers loaded the boys' bags into the car, he stood off to the side, trying to avoid people watching him swipe big fat teardrops with his fist as they ran down his cheeks. There were so many emotions to process, and he felt overwhelmed.

He also felt strange. He had expected to feel nothing but happiness upon being reunited with his mother after eighty-one days apart, but he actually felt a range of emotions and couldn't make sense of the fact that many of them seemed to be in conflict with each other. Nobody had told Yordy that he might miss Mamá Sobeida, his foster mother, or the other boys with whom he and Fernando had lived. He hadn't really had enough time to experience closure with them. The same was true of the staff at Cayuga Centers. The news made the agency out to be one of the "bad guys" in the story of family separation, but Yordy's experience was entirely positive, and he had formed attachments to some of the teachers and workers. What about the girl he liked? Would he ever see her again?

And no one had prepared him for the rush of relief he would feel at no longer being the sole person responsible for Fernando's safety and well-being, though the coming weeks and months would be filled with tense moments as he struggled to establish a new identity as a big brother, rather than a father and mother figure rolled up into one vulnerable teenager. While in foster care, Yordy would enfold Fernando in his arms at night as they slept together in a twin bed, and he was always vigilant about Fernando's needs. Shedding that role and settling into the identity of just being a kid himself was going to be surprisingly hard. Within a few months, he'd also have to figure out what it meant to be an immigrant teenage boy who spoke little English in a New York City public school.

Fernando's transition was also going to be challenging. From the moment he had been separated from his mother in Arizona, dressed in a gray sweat suit, and put on a plane to New York, he had clung to Yordy and relied upon his big brother to be his protector and his comfort. Now that their mother was back in the picture, Fernando felt hypervigilant and terrified to let her out of his sight. Rosayra's other children had, perhaps, grown accustomed to living without her for long periods of time. But for Fernando, she had been a constant presence in his life, and he guarded against any relationship or activity that might separate them again, even momentarily. He chafed against Yordy's fatherlike directives and ultimatums, telling him that their mother was back. Ultimately, however, his adjustment would be easier than Yordy's, and easier than Rosayra's, too. She struggled with her own challenges, including when and how to assert authority. She felt guilty for the separation, and the guilt made her reluctant to chastise or correct Fernando at moments when he could have used more guidance.

It would take a full year before they all finally began to settle into comfortable roles, but even then, there would be moments when the trauma they had suffered would peek through, causing strain.

From Cayuga, the family was taken to their new, temporary home in Park Slope, an upscale neighborhood in Brooklyn. The streets were lined with trees, there were restaurants and shops less than a block away, and the residential side streets were as clean and peaceful as could be. Neighbors walking dogs or taking out the trash were friendly and waved or said hello. A playground was just around the corner, and the nearest subway station and library were a short walk away, too. The family couldn't have found a more pleasant place to live if they had tried—and if they had, it would have been far beyond their means. Average rent in Brooklyn is $2,700 per month.

A group of IFT's New York volunteers and a group of Beth Elohim congregants gathered at the house for a welcome party. Summer sunlight flooded through the large windows of the living room and kitchen, and organizers laid out a spread of food on the marble counter, inviting everyone to take a plate and serve themselves. Fresh berries and grapes, pasta salad, and pizza sat alongside a heaping platter of that quintessential New York staple: bagels and cream cheese.

Rosayra and the boys were like celebrities, greeted with hearty handshakes and big bear hugs, and "Congratulations!" and "We're so glad you're here!" As guests tested out their Spanish, a couple members of IFT and the Refugee Task Force, Beth Elohim's rabbi, and her colleague Rabbi Stephanie Kolin of Manhattan's Central Synagogue (now at Union Temple of Brooklyn) gathered with me and moved to the living room, where we spread ourselves out on the floor and urged each other to dream big. How many mothers could we get out? What else needed to be done? How could we do more? Who could we connect with to widen and strengthen the net of support we had woven hastily?

It was World Cup season, and Rabbi Timoner's son, Benji, invited Yordy to step out of the welcome party and walk a few houses down to watch a match with some friends. Both Yordy and Rosayra seemed a little wary to separate again so soon, but the twin temptations of soccer and game-day snacks were too great. He returned a few hours later, chuffed about the game and his new friends, one of whom shared his birthday. They would celebrate together a few weeks later.

This *is the beloved community*, I thought to myself, as I looked around and took everything in, *this group of people who just shows up, right where they are, with whatever they have, saying "How can I help? How can I be a force for making this better?"* In the Jewish faith, in the Hebrew language, there is a word that sums up what was happening there that day, a word I would learn later, when Rabbi Kolin offered a Rosh Hashanah sermon. The word is *hineini* and means "Here I am." The word made me think about the lyrics of one of my favorite folksongs that I learned growing up in the Catholic Church, one I taught myself to play on the piano because I loved it so much:

> *Here I am, Lord. Is it I, Lord?*
> *I have heard you calling in the night.*
> *I will go, Lord, if you lead me.*
> *I will hold your people in my heart.*

Though I hadn't stepped into a church as a congregant in years, the words were on instant recall. They were a guiding light.

Hineini. Here I am. Here *we* are. That's really what this is all about, just showing up. Showing up with what we have, where we are. It seems so simple, but it's incredibly profound and powerful. We are the ones we have been waiting for. As Rabbi Kolin explained in her sermon, "The power of saying the word *hineini* is enough to change the course of history. It's enough to heal profound suffering for one single person, or for the whole world. It's a legacy given to us by our tradition. When our name is called, we are a people who respond: *Hineini.*"

———

Hineini was not the only word or concept that Rosayra and I would learn about from our new friends in the months ahead. Rosayra, who is an evangelical Christian, and I, the lapsed Catholic, were also introduced to the notion of *tikkun olam*. Rabbi Timoner explained it simply: *tikkun olam* is about repairing the world. And the work of repairing the world doesn't fall upon God. It falls upon us. It involves acts of loving kindness and humanity, and performing practical, tangible actions that promote *tzedakah*, or justice and righteousness. These are the responsibilities of someone who understands and accepts his or her obligation to help repair the world.

The months of separation were hard for Rosayra and her family, both for her sons here in the United States, and for her extended family in Guatemala, who felt so afraid for her and the boys, as well as powerless to do anything to help them. They were also hard for those of us opposed to the Trump Administration's immigration policies and procedures, hard for those of us who feared the xenophobia that seemed to be enjoying free reign. We were all exhausted, physically and emotionally, and, yes, spiritually, too.

Where was God or the divine at that moment? Where was God on the border? Or in detention centers? If I had asked her, Rabbi Kolin probably would have smiled and told me that God was right there with us, all the time. Rosayra would have said that, too. "The barrage of things coming at us all at once is not going to let up soon," Rabbi Kolin said in her Rosh Hashanah sermon. "That is both the nature of life as well as this historical moment in which we are living. But in our own hands," she continued, "is the healing of our souls, our homes, and our world."

PART
III

14

Bittersweet Season

Our summer in Brooklyn is a beautiful but strange chapter of my life that I will never forget. When you dream of being re-united with your children after having been pulled apart from them, that version of the reunion is painted in a golden light and everything is beautiful. The mind is eager to ward off any pos-sibility that it could be otherwise. So, I am unprepared, the first morning that we wake up in this gorgeous, borrowed home in Brooklyn, given to us so kindly for a period of time, to feel any-thing other than happiness.

It is odd and it catches me by surprise, the feeling of hap-piness mixed with longing and sadness that overtakes me. I am with my boys. We have made it, finally, to the country where I believe we will be safe, and where we will have a fair chance to file for asylum and make a case for why we should remain here. Seeing the boys pad to the kitchen in their paja-mas, their hair tousled, their eyes sleepy, makes me so grateful for the support of the many people who made this moment possible. It is a joy to cook breakfast for them for the first time in months.

And yet, before I sit down to eat with them, I have to excuse myself for a moment and go in the next room to dab my eyes with a tissue. Standing at the stove, I'd become overcome with memories of Guatemala, memories of cooking breakfast for the boys and their sisters, all of us gathered to eat at the table with my mother. I don't want Yordy and Fernando to see me crying. I don't want them to think that I am anything other than happy. Life is full of challenges and obstacles, I tell myself, trying to make myself strong enough to smile and go sit with the boys. Only God will give us the strength to keep going.

When we finish eating, we wash the dishes and take time to begin talking about our experiences over the months that we have been apart. Those conversations, in which we so often find ourselves crying, are often interrupted, as people come to visit us. When they say goodbye, leaving us to ourselves again, I tell Yordy how proud I am of him for taking so much responsibility for his brother, for explaining to Fernando why we were apart in an age-appropriate way that he could understand. Yordy beams with pride, but I catch him expressing frustration, too. Just as Fernando doesn't want to be apart from me—he often runs up to me and wraps his arms around my legs, saying, "I love you so much! I don't want you to go away!"—he doesn't want to be apart from Yordy, either. Rabbi Timoner's son and Yordy are becoming friends, and Fernando cries if they want "big boy" time without him. He begs Yordy to come back soon and melts into a temper tantrum.

To be honest, I'm not entirely prepared for these emotions, each of us struggling with reactions to our reunion that we didn't expect. We each have fears and anxieties. I find that it is hard, at first, to get Yordy to leave the house, even if we are going out to explore the neighborhood together. The volunteers from the synagogue are a blessing, especially Bonnie. They give me information about school and help me set up doctors' appointments for the boys, and they help us all get into therapy, which helps us enormously. Bonnie is so concerned about us, and she visits frequently, often with her children, who form a close bond with Fernando. I am grateful for the children's patience with Fernando, especially since his behavior isn't the best. He yells a lot, he's demanding, and he wants to control everything in a play situation. Bonnie's children are so accommodating and tender with him, as if they have an intuitive understanding that he is a broken boy who is trying to put himself back together.

One day, we take a long subway ride from Brooklyn to the Bronx, where Yordy has an appointment with a cardiologist. While in foster care, doctors discovered during a routine medical exam that he has a heart murmur, and he needs additional evaluations. The hospital, he says, is close to where Mamá Sobeida lives, and he asks whether we can go see her. I say yes, even though he has used Mamá Sobeida to wound me more than once since we have been reunited. Sometimes, when I ask him to do something or tell him something that doesn't sit well with him, he says, "Mamá Sobeida wouldn't ask me to do that!" He has always known how to push my buttons.

Still, I know that this behavior is just his way of trying to make sense of what has happened to him, to us, and I welcome the opportunity to meet and thank Mamá Sobeida. Yordy and Fernando have both told me about how lovingly she took care of them. We get to her building, and Fernando says, "It's the fifth floor." We climb the stairs to her apartment, and he runs to her door in excitement. Yordy rings the doorbell. Mamá Sobeida opens the door and bursts into tears. So do I.

We later learn that we aren't supposed to see her—the terms of her agreement as a foster parent are that she not have contact with a child or the biological family once the child is no longer in her care—but the encounter is a positive one for all of us. I am able to speak with her and tell her how grateful I am for her kindness and her care. Months from now, she will call me, weeping, to tell me that one of the boys who lived with her when she had Yordy and Fernando has been killed in a car accident. I will cry along with her, weighed down by the pain of thinking how that child's mother must have fled violence, like I did, only for her child to die here. It seems terribly unjust, even if it is, as I believe it must be, part of God's plan.

Summer in New York is a beautiful time, and our friends show us the best of the city. They take us to Sunset Park, where many Latinos live and food trucks serve food from all over the Americas. Between legal and medical appointments, we swim, ride bikes, and go to barbecues and backyard parties. We become confident—mostly—about using the subway, and we use it to explore Brooklyn and Manhattan, making our own maps of the city with each new experience and memory.

———

August draws to a close. The family that loaned us this enormous, beautiful, peaceful home is returning soon, so it's time for us to move. Immigrant Families Together has found us a new place to live. After Vicky, a woman on Manhattan's Upper East Side, heard Julie in a radio interview, she tracked her down and let Julie know that she wanted to help. Vicky is divorced, and her adult sons live on their own. She has two apartments in the same building: she lives in one and keeps the other one for her sons' occasional visits or for other guests. Some years earlier, she had opened up the apartment that we will be living in to people who were left homeless by a hurricane in Louisiana. They had lived there for months. She won't charge us rent, and she doesn't have a time limit on how long we can stay. "Let's just see how it goes," she says.

We spend our last weekend in Brooklyn packing our things into bags and boxes. It's so much that we end up needing two cars to move from Park Slope to Manhattan. Nearly everything we've acquired since July has been donated or given to us as gifts. There are boxes of books and toys, and bags and bags of shoes and clothing. Fernando has become the owner of two soccer balls, a bike, and I don't know how many board games and puzzles. We don't need all of it, but people keep offering these gifts, usually with an embarrassed apology, asking us to forgive them for how we have been treated. The generosity is immense. Sometimes, it's actually overwhelming.

Our time in Brooklyn has been a profound blessing. In the ample space of our temporary home, my sons and I were able to begin the work of healing, of rebuilding our family. It has not been easy work. The separation has left us all with enormous amounts of emotional debris. We are impatient, anxious, and insecure. We are uncertain of ourselves and one another, and how to relate to each other after such a painful time apart. I wonder how long it will take us to clean it all out, to remove the cobwebs and dust that gathered in the corners of our souls, and to scrub off the crusty scales that grew to protect our most tender places.

For all of my gratitude—and I am speechless when it comes to knowing the words to express my appreciation for this home and the incredible people of Beth Elohim, people who, despite having a different religion, have become part of our family—I have spent some restless days here. People have been so kind and so good that it has been easy to rely upon them and to forget about the work I need to do on myself. When you're no longer in detention, you say, "Oh, let me call this person and ask them to help me." But in detention, you have no one but God to help you. He will always give you the best of Himself. When you are out in the world, there's so much that can get in the way of seeing and remembering that. I have to bring myself back to that idea over and over again.

When I left detention, when I was together with my boys

again and we were in Brooklyn, I felt my spiritual life begin to dry up. I would try to read the Bible, but it just didn't capture my attention the way that it had when I was in Eloy. I'd say, "I'm going to read," as if saying so would make it so, but I just couldn't. I was uttering the laziest, simplest prayers. I had a roof, I had food. I thought I was fine.

But the spirit . . . the spirit is always going to ask for what it needs, and the spirit is nurtured through words. I had everything I needed and I was with my children, but when I got here, I kept thinking, *Oh, I'm here now. My fight is over.* My mind said, *Hey, relax. Go surf on Facebook.* But my spirit said, *Go to your prayer corner. Go read the Bible.* My spirit led me to these people of the Jewish faith, who shared their beliefs with me and showed me how much we have in common.

In a short time, our Beth Elohim friends have given so much of themselves to us and we have learned so much from them about living our faith in our daily lives, about being the kind of believers I read about in those verses from the book of Matthew back when I was in Eloy. It's amazing to me, the kindnesses and support they have extended to us as acts of their own faith, and it's a reminder to me that it doesn't matter what church you attend, whether you are Catholic or evangelical or Jewish—that's a focus of people; that's not God's focus. God said, "Go and preach. The one who shares my word will prosper." Our Beth Elohim friends shared their word through their deeds. It is my greatest hope that God will bless them and they will continue to prosper and help other people.

———

When we arrive at the new apartment, a doorman dressed in a suit with gold-colored buttons and a hat with matching gilded trim steps out of the building with a wheeled cart. Fernando is duly impressed. The doorman lifts the boxes and bags onto the cart and welcomes us, saying that he's happy we're here. It's as if we are honored guests checking into a luxurious hotel, and he has been directed to treat us with exceptional courtesy. A few months from now, around Christmas, he will have become such a familiar fixture of our daily lives in New York that he will give Fernando a race car, one of his favorite kinds of toys, as a gift. Now, though, he is friendly but formal, and he tells us to go on up to the eighteenth floor; he will bring the overloaded cart in a few minutes.

The elevator doors open and our new host, Vicky, greets us, taking us on a tour of the apartment, our new home. It is so high in the sky, with so many windows, and the rooms are flooded with sunlight. A miniature jungle of plants fills the living room windowsill. Masks that look as if they have come from all parts of the world hang on the wall. Some of them are frightening, and Fernando recoils at the sight of them. Yordy, Fernando, and I each have our own room and our own bed, and each offers a different view of the city. Vicky opens closet doors and shows us extra pillows, extra comforters, just in case we get cold. She opens another closet and shows Fernando a treasure trove of Legos, promising that when her sons come to visit, she will ask them to show him their special train set, too.

Then, she takes us up a set of stairs that connects the apartment where we will be living to her apartment, which is right above ours. She tells us that we are welcome to use her kitchen and that we can come up here any time if we want to access the balcony, which is long and wraps around two sides of her apartment, offering views to the south and the west. Like our windowsill, the balcony is a tangle of plants, and I feel a sense of warmth, despite the fact that there's a hint of autumnal chill in the air, because I have the feeling that Vicky and I are going to become good friends.

After we unload everything at the new apartment, we are tired, but Vicky asks whether we want to go to the park with her the next morning. She doesn't speak Spanish and I don't speak English, so we communicate via Google Translate. She explains that she belongs to a club whose members go foraging for mushrooms together, tromping around the less-visited spots of the city's public parks to look for edible fungi. Mushroom hunting in New York City, this metropolis of concrete and skyscrapers? I'm definitely intrigued and we love nature, so I say, yes, we'll accept her invitation. She says she'll pack a picnic lunch and we'll make a whole day of it.

This is the first of many adventures that we will enjoy with Vicky and, when they come to visit, her sons, who, among other things, will teach us how to ice skate—or try to! The mushroom foraging trip is wildly successful. It turns out, much to the surprise of Vicky and the members of the mushroom club, that Yordy and Fernando are expert fungi finders. They only needed a quick lesson to identify the edible specimens before scrambling off and returning with a basketful of mushrooms, more than those that were found by all of the more experienced members of the club. We will take these home and clean them, and Vicky will turn them into wondrous dishes, including mushroom ice cream! The boys' find so excites Vicky and the mushroom club members that she gives them a membership to the club for Christmas.

We settle into a companionable life with Vicky, sharing dishes we each make with one another, as well as the news of our days. Vicky, who describes herself as a Jewish atheist, texts Julie to say that even though she doesn't believe in God, she thinks God put us in her life for a reason. I am a believer, of course, and I feel the same way. God has put the most amazing people in our lives, and regardless of how long we live with her, she will always be an important member of our growing chosen family.

15

School Days

Our move from Brooklyn to the Upper East Side of Manhattan introduces other changes, too, though these aren't solely a function of geography, but of the season. It is September, which means it's time for Yordy and Fernando to start school. Vicky, who is a college professor and administrator, helps us navigate the confusing enrollment process, and Fernando is admitted to a wonderful public school just a couple of blocks from our apartment. The principal herself gives us a tour of the school and emphasizes her commitment to our family. At the end of our meeting, she gives Fernando a bag full of books.

Yordy, meanwhile, is admitted to a high school near Union Square, a school that's specifically for teens who come from other countries. The international school is characterized by its incredibly diverse student body, and in his first days there, Yordy will come home and tell me about his peers, who speak every language imaginable: Russian and Arabic, Chinese and Indian languages, and Spanish. Somehow, though they all lack English fluency, they learn how to communicate with each other and with their teachers, who speak to them and provide instruction only in English.

Back-to-school season means changes for me, too. I'm not allowed to work legally yet—asylum seekers have a year to file their asylum application, and they can't submit a request for a work permit until they've filed for asylum—so although I have legal, medical, and mental health appointments, I also have time to fill. While attending the first open house at Yordy's school, I make the impromptu decision to run for the position of PTA co-president. I'd held the same position in Guatemala; why not here? I throw my name into the ring and I'm shocked when I'm unanimously voted in as PTA co-president for the 2018–2019 school year. Yordy's school also offers ESL classes, so I register for those. I'll struggle through the classes and even contemplate dropping out, but I push through, showing up each Tuesday evening, even when it's unbearably cold, or snowing, or raining.

This is the immigrant experience I wish people could see, not because it's *my* experience, but because it's the story of so many of us, coming to the United States to escape violence and to build lives in which we will contribute fully to society. We are grateful for any support, but we're not waiting for a handout. We want to be part of *your* American dream. We want to help you realize it. We want to share in it with you.

In late winter, parent-teacher conferences are scheduled and the hope of spring is tantalizingly close. I can't wait to see the spring flowers push out of the cold soil, opening boldly to announce the new season. I receive the notices about the days and times I should meet Yordy's and Fernando's teachers, and I bundle up in my coat, scarf, hat, and gloves, hoping I can store all of these away soon.

Yordy's teachers sing his praises. He struggles, they say, but he tries hard and has promise. His big class presentation, which he had to develop and present on a computer, was the best among all his peers. He dressed in a suit bought by Immigrant Families Together and had perfected the presentation by running through it with the organization's volunteers, making sure his information was accurate and that everything made sense. A few weeks after the parent-teacher conference, he is awarded two certificates—one for perfect attendance and one for being a model citizen. He isn't bullied and he is not in danger here; I feel like I can see a literal weight lifted off his shoulders.

Fernando is also doing well in school, so well that I can hardly believe it. This boy—who had so much difficulty letting me out of his sight once we were reunited, and who had even more trouble letting Yordy out of his sight since Yordy had cared for him more like a father than an older brother—is thrilled to wake up and join his kindergarten classmates for days of fun and learning. He has even asked me whether he can walk to school alone, asserting that he is a big boy, that the streets are safe, and that he knows how to get from home to school!

His teacher tells me, through a translator, that he is a joy in the classroom. He is kind to his friends and takes great pleasure in helping others. He tries hard and doesn't give up, even when lessons are hard for him. She is impressed by how quickly he has picked up English and how rich his vocabulary has become. I am, too, but it didn't come without a price—specifically a $100 cable bill that he ran up when he bought *Hotel Transylvania* on pay-per-view, watching it dozens of times. I tell her that I chuckle because he comes home and tells me sternly, wagging his finger in my face, "You must learn English, and if you don't, I won't be able to talk with you anymore. We speak Spanish when we are in Guatemala and English when we are in the United States." He doesn't know that it's harder for adults to learn new things than it is for children, who are still so new to the world and its ways.

It hurts me that my sons can't enjoy this success and safety in the country where they were born, and it hurts me, too, that my daughters are so far away and that they can't benefit from such good schools and a safe, nurturing environment. But when I think of all the boys have accomplished here in such a short time, and how much more they can accomplish with time and support, I beam with pride and feel that, yes, my decision to make the difficult, dangerous journey that brought us here was the right one for us.

16

The Horizon

Those of us who are immigrants live in an in-between space. We belong neither there, where we came from, nor here, where we find ourselves now. And yet, we belong to both. We are from one place, now living in another. We walk with each foot in a separate world, a circumstance that requires considerable skill. No matter how long we live in our adopted country, and no matter how warmly we are embraced and how comfortable we are, we will always be aware that we are of some other place, that we were forged in conditions that are hard, if not impossible, for our new friends to understand, and that we are growing and evolving in a place that is difficult, if not impossible, for our blood families to know or comprehend.

This is especially true for asylum seekers, who are in total limbo. Our cases aren't yet resolved. Decisions about our futures have not yet been rendered. We want to start building lives here—we *have* started building lives here—but we do so tentatively, both yearning and afraid to strengthen and solidify friendships and connections, lest we be torn from them suddenly. We put down our fragile roots, allowing them to settle in the soil, aware that they could be ripped up at any time. We open our hearts to others but feel ourselves holding back a bit. The heart is a resilient muscle, but it is also a tender one.

———

On April 15, 2019, just a year after we arrived in the United States, I am scheduled to appear before the immigration court for my final hearing. Yordy, Fernando, and I wake up early. They won't go to school today. Instead, we will all dress in our best clothes and go downtown together, where I will appear before a judge who will decide whether I can remain in the United States or whether I will be sent back to Guatemala. By the end of the day, my fate will be known, even if Yordy's and Fernando's fates will remain unresolved. Attorneys determined that my case and the boys' cases should remain separate.

As I button my blouse and choose the earrings and necklace I'll wear, I try not to think about the fact that our cases could have different outcomes. The boys' lawyer and my lawyer have both tried to prepare us for this possibility: that I could be granted asylum and they could be deported, or they could be granted asylum and I could be deported. I don't know what I'd do in either scenario, even though I know that whatever happens will be God's will. I can only hope that His plan is to keep us all here and that, with time, I can bring Britny and Dulce here as well.

The waiting room outside the courtroom is full. I see a couple of people I don't recognize, and I think they must be waiting for their hearings, too, because they look as anxious as I feel. The rest of the people here are our friends. There's Bonnie from Brooklyn, for whom I will always be grateful. She was there on our first day in New York, and she has been there for us ever since, always concerned about our well-being. Vicky, the owner of our apartment, a generous host, and someone I have come to think of as my American mother because we have grown so close, has come, too, rearranging her work schedule to be here for us. I am especially grateful that she is here because she had an accident recently and her arm is in a big, bulky foam cast that frustrates her because she is such an active woman. Julie and Francisco and several other Immigrant Families Together volunteers have come to support us as well. Julie takes advantage of the wait to run upstairs to the ninth floor, where she drops off paperwork for the organization's latest bond payment.

We all stand around in an uncomfortable silence. I'm nervous, and I know everyone else is, too. No one knows what to say, including me, and so we just watch the clock and wonder what's taking so long for my case to be called.

I'm the next name on the docket. I stand up, smooth my skirt, and follow my lawyer into the courtroom. What happens next isn't what I expected at all. I've been envisioning this moment for months, trying to anticipate how I would feel, what I would say, how I would calm my nerves, and how I would maintain my composure when the decision was handed down by the judge, no matter what that decision was. But the judge says that because of some scheduling problems and a clerical error, he can't hear my case today. I have to come back again . . . in October.

Some people might be elated with such an outcome, but I am crushed. The delay pushes back so many plans, or may force me to reconsider them entirely. We were going to move to our own apartment, but I wonder now whether we should remain with Vicky until our cases are resolved. An October court date also means that should the asylum decision not be in my favor, the boys' schooling will be disrupted in some way.

Five more months of limbo stretch out before me. I know they will go fast, since life here is busy and time really does seem to fly. But for Britny and Dulce, who had hoped to have some sort of clarity about their own futures with my asylum decided, those five months will likely seem as long as five years. I leave the courtroom dreading my nightly phone call with them. Somehow, I will have to find the words to tell them that I don't know when we can be together again.

I look at Yordy and Fernando. Yordy is wearing the same suit he wore for his school presentation, his white dress shirt pressed and accented with a blue and red plaid bow tie. I watched him this morning out of the corner of my eye as he slicked his hair until it was gleaming, fussing until he got it just right. I'm struck by how handsome he has become, a young man with his whole life spread out ahead of him. I feel excited about his future, and I know he does, too. Just last week, he gave a speech at a gala hosted by The Door, the legal clinic where his and Fernando's attorney works. As he spoke, I looked around the room and saw how people were riveted by his words, and when he finished, they rushed up to shake his hand or give him a hug and congratulate him. He says now that he wants to be a lawyer, too, though he also has other interests and dreams. He loves cooking, and he's good at it. When we visit Julie, Francisco, and their kids, he grabs an apron, ties it around his waist, and helps out in the kitchen. Francisco has become a father figure to him, and they talk about life and Yordy's plans for the future as they cook. Who knows what he could become with a good education and the support we have here?

Looking at Fernando in his suit, I can see how much he has grown, too! Though he's a picky eater and often tries to skip meals altogether, he is taller and more filled out than he was this time last year. Now, I can barely carry him home when he falls asleep on the subway or the bus. There are other changes, too, and when I stop to think about it, I find it hard to process them all. His English fluency is amazing and makes me so proud, as does the fact that the school reports that he is a model student. His report cards are in English, and I don't understand the numbers and what they mean, nor the long paragraphs of comments describing Fernando's progress in each subject. Julie sits down and reads them to me, translating them into Spanish so that I can understand the full scope of his achievements.

"He's doing well in every subject, and he just needs to practice and grow in the same areas that all of his classmates need to practice and grow," she explains. "He cares about others, and he shares, and he's a good listener, and he always tries hard." Sometimes, she pauses for a long while, seeming to hold back tears. "Every single comment is positive, Rosy. I'm so proud of him," she says. *If this is what he can accomplish in just one year*, I think to myself, *imagine how much he will have learned by this time next year, or five years from now. Imagine what he has the possibility of becoming!*

———

When separated moms are released from detention centers by Immigrant Families Together, Francisco often asks them the question, What was your plan? He means, he has explained to me, this: When you were in your home country, contemplating the journey to the United States, what did you think you'd do once you got here? Where did you think you'd live, and how did you expect to support yourself? What did you envision for your children? How did you imagine the shape of your days would look? In short, what did you believe the future would hold for you and your children?

Although he is a refugee, too, and he shares that experience of leaving a home and making another one in a foreign place, he always seems surprised when a woman responds that she doesn't know. Her vision spread only to the horizon: the border. Beyond the border, life is a blank slate. Sure, perhaps she expects to live with a family member and hopes that they will provide for her and her children's needs until she can get on her feet, but she can't see her days or envision how they will be filled. So accustomed to living in survival mode, it might be impossible for her to see what she and her children could become. Her ability to see the future is constrained because she has no frame of reference for imagining life beyond the border, no way to envision herself and the contours of her daily life when she is mired in an environment of blinding fear.

When she is in her home country and thinking of leaving, she also can't imagine the good people she will meet, the ones who will help her and her children along the way. The support they will give might exceed her wildest dreams, and it might begin to mold her and her children into confident, excited people who are living without fear for the first time in their lives. This transformation makes them bold and brave, ready to try new things, ready to try on the skin of the people they could become.

Yordy and Fernando have both been spreading their wings, and even when this terrifies or bewilders me, I keep my fears to myself—well, mostly—and cheer them on. Yordy goes on a retreat with the church youth group over a long weekend. The trip takes them miles away, to another state! As if that's not enough to rattle my nerves, the trip organizers and chaperones tell the kids that they have to turn in their phones at the beginning of the retreat—they have to learn how to be together without technology as a mediator. I like this idea in theory, as Yordy spends far too much time on his phone, but when it means that I can't communicate with him, I get anxious. I keep wanting to send him a text, to check in and see how he's doing, but every time I pull up his name on my phone, I realize he won't receive the message until the end of the trip, and so I put the phone down and just pray instead. I toss and turn in my bed at night, hoping that he's having fun and that he's safe, but I know I won't really rest until he's back in New York.

When he returns, Yordy is barely recognizable as my child. I have never seen him so excited, so alive! He tells me about all the new activities he tried, including building a campfire and making something called s'mores, and about the counselors and a concert that capped off the weekend. He says that they're going to have another retreat in the summer, once school's out, and he's so excited about going that he said yes without asking me first.

I feel a twinge of sadness about this, but mostly, I feel proud. The young man Yordy is becoming will have so many opportunities, so many possibilities. My role as his mother is changing. With each day that passes, I am no longer the person who will make his decisions for him. Instead, I am learning to let him make his own decisions, moving into a role in which I support the choices he makes for himself. This is a little scary for both of us, and we each fumble a bit as we try to settle comfortably into these new roles, but I can see the road ahead beginning to reveal itself. If he is granted asylum, he will stay here, finish high school, and go on to college. He will enter a career that he wants for himself, not just taking the only job that's available to him. And, I like to imagine that one day, he will find a way to pay this all forward, to take the security and confidence and opportunities that have been given to him and share them with someone else who needs them just as much as he did.

Fernando has turned six years old, but I feel as if he's going on sixteen, or even twenty-six. He negotiates his own play dates in English with his friends' parents, telling them, "My mom's English isn't very good yet, but she's trying"; and he acts as translator between us, not asking whether a day and time are good for me, but *telling* me that he's locked in the get-together on his calendar. While I often feel helpless because I can't communicate more easily or independently with people who speak only English, I also have to laugh at my little social butterfly and event coordinator, who doesn't exhibit the least bit of social anxiety. As the school year comes to a close, he is able to read and translate the notes that are sent home in English, and he lets me know about a "moving up" party that will mark his transition from kindergarten to first grade. At the party, he sings songs in English and talks nonstop to his friends and their parents, and I watch it all with wonder and pride. This child I first brought to the United States still suckling at my breast, who depended upon me entirely, is now navigating his world with the greatest of ease. It's more than I ever could have imagined.

Each night, I call home to Guatemala. I speak to my mother and ask her how her day has gone. I ask about my brothers and sisters and, of course, my daughters. My mother and sister worry that school and marimba lessons don't fill enough time to keep the girls out of danger, and, they hesitate to tell me, trouble seems to be brewing in our hometown again. Just a few nights ago, my mother confesses, someone climbed onto the top of her house and tried to peel back the flimsy laminate roofing. She worries that extortion calls will start anew. The would-be intruder made her so fearful that it caused her to have a strokelike episode, and she has been hospitalized. Thousands of miles away, I feel sick with concern and guilty about my inability to help her or protect her. God willing, I will be able to work soon and help reinforce the roof. And I hope, too, that I will be able to get my girls out of Guatemala and bring them to my side. I want to see them blossom just as I see Yordy and Fernando growing and flourishing.

———

Sometimes, before we go to bed, Yordy and I stand in front of the south-facing window of Vicky's eighteenth-floor apartment and look out over the city. They say New York is the city that never sleeps, and we can see why. No matter the hour, we always see taxis and cars headed down Second Avenue, their drivers honking horns as if it were noon and everyone was awake. The skyline never goes dark; lights always glisten through the night, keeping us company until morning comes.

Before we say good-night, Yordy and I reminisce about our other home, Guatemala, and about what brought us here and what that journey was like for us. We don't leave out the hard parts, but we tend to focus on the beautiful ones—all the moments of grateful surprise, when someone extended a hand to us and asked whether they could be part of our journey. We talk about our good luck, and our friends, and then we pray, asking God to keep them all in His kingdom. Just before we drift off to sleep, I think about the mothers in Eloy and other detention centers. Where are they now? How are they? Are their children okay?

I think about the mothers who are setting off on their journeys north, babies tied to their backs or children's hands in theirs, leading them away from home, probably forever. Then, I fall asleep and dream about the ones who are getting close to the border, the ones spending their last night outside the United States, out in the cold. In my dream, I talk to God directly: "Cover them, Lord, with your love. Let them, as you have let us, have a chance to live. Let them know your mercy and your grace. Amen."

Epilogue

The day before Rosy's final hearing had been one of those early autumn, brilliant blue-sky days that still feel like summer. The temperature had risen to 91 degrees at the hottest part of the day, and Rosy was sweating as she stood in the courtyard of Fernando's school, waiting for him to be dismissed. When he bounded out of the door and onto the artificial turf, she hugged him and peeled his sweater off as he complained about the heat. Through Google Translate, she reminded his teacher that Fernando would miss school the next day, as she had a court appointment and her sons were required to be present.

"Let's go home," she urged Fernando, who wanted to enjoy summer's last stand by spending an hour or so in the shady playground just down the street. He hoped to glimpse his friend, Sophie, of whom he had become so fond the year before. They were no longer in the same class since, as he liked to say in English, "I met all the challenges of kindergarten and now I am in a new class in first grade." If Sophie came to the playground, too, they could swing on the high bars of the jungle gym, or chase each other, or just sit and talk in the cool shadows cast by the tall London planetrees.

"Please," he begged, drawing out the "s" and the "e" for extra persuasive emphasis. Rosy didn't like to say no to her children, but she had to be firm. "Tomorrow is a big day, and we need to rest." Since they had moved to their own apartment, the commute to and from school had become significantly longer, so she had to factor that into many decisions she made now.

Mainly, though, she was conscious of the time. In less than twenty-four hours, she would be sitting in a courtroom, awaiting her fate as a judge determined whether to grant or deny her asylum request. There was still so much she needed to do to get ready for court: make the boys try on their suits one last time to ensure they still fit, iron their button-down shirts and her own outfit, and inspect everyone's shoes to make sure they were shiny.

She always enjoyed dressing well, regardless of the occasion, but she knew that making a visual impression in court could influence, even if only slightly, the outcome of her case. A well-dressed family, she thought, conveyed to a judge that they understood the gravity of the law. It demonstrated their respect for the court, for the judge, even for the United States itself. She knew that dressing well also suggested that the family was put together enough that they wouldn't become what the court urged so much against: immigrants becoming a public charge . . . a burden on society. Most of the clothes were donated, true. So were her black heels, which fit her perfectly and looked as though they'd never been worn. But as she smoothed the boys' lapels and tied the bow on the collar of her blouse, she knew the judge wouldn't know the clothes had been donated. He'd just know they looked kempt, and Rosy knew that to look otherwise would do them no favors.

————

Thursday, October 3, dawned gray, damp, and chilly, as if asserting that summer had decided to retire for the year. "Yesterday, you could have worn your bathing suit, but today it's practically winter coat weather. We'll get up to a high of 50 degrees today," the radio announcer said, adding, "and be sure to take your umbrella with you. It's going to be a cloudy one, with lots of rain."

I pulled our kids' raincoats off their hangers. As they put their coats on, I reminded them that a sitter would be picking them up from school. "Are you going to Immigration?" our youngest one asked. "Yes, today is Rosy's hearing," I replied. "Give her a hug," Olivia said, "a really BIG one!" After I dropped them off at school, I returned home to dress for the hearing before driving downtown with Francisco. I looked out our bedroom window and contemplated what to wear. I hadn't yet taken any of my fall and winter clothes out of storage, and nothing hanging in front of me looked right. *The weather seemed ominous*, I thought, but I refused to say anything about this aloud. After all, it was Rosy who had told me almost a year earlier, as the chill of fall settled on New York, that she loved all weather—sun and clouds, rain and snow, hot and cold, all of it—as long as she was free. As I pulled on a sweater and straightened it out over my shoulders, I hoped that Rosy wasn't feeling the same way I was about the heavy, dark clouds that were gathering over the city.

Despite the radio announcer's admonition to take an umbrella, Francisco and I couldn't find ours, and we dashed through the rain to meet Rosy and the boys at a coffee shop before walking together to the federal building, where her attorney, several of her friends, and IFT volunteers were waiting. At 1 p.m., when the courtroom opened, we all filed in and took our places on wooden benches, waiting for the hearing to begin. The Department of Homeland Security attorney, always identifiable because they push a two-tiered cart carrying baskets piled high with overstuffed brown file folders, bumbled into the courtroom. Frankly, he looked a bit disheveled. Unlike his colleagues, whose folders tended to be orderly, stacked neatly in the baskets, his folders were a right mess, their contents spilling out of them, corners of pages bent and askew. He also had a tangle of plastic bags sitting beneath the towering, precarious pile. Torn bits of Bubble Wrap were taped onto the sides of the cart, and it wasn't obvious what these were for, either; they weren't affixed to the cart's handle.

The attorney himself almost seemed held together by tape. His worn, ill-fitting suit had a long, ragged thread sneaking out of the lining. He wore a pair of black slip-on Skechers.

When the judge called the session to order, he seemed surprised by the number of people in the courtroom—the benches were almost full—and he asked, through a court interpreter, if Rosy wanted all of us to remain for the hearing. "Yes, Judge," she replied. He asked the potential witnesses—an expert who could speak about conditions in Guatemala, including the subject of gangs, whose $1,000 fee had been paid for by friends; her therapist; and her boys—to step out of the courtroom and into the waiting room; they would be called upon if needed, but were not allowed to listen to Rosy's own testimony.

Before the judge could swear Rosy in, the DHS attorney asked for a sidebar. *Not good*, I thought to myself, trying to make my face blank. I didn't want Rosy to look at me and feel fear. The judge assented, inviting both attorneys into his chambers. Those of us left in the courtroom waited twenty-five minutes for everyone to emerge and for the judge to go on the record and swear Rosy in.

After the swearing in, the judge reviewed Rosy's asylum file with the attorneys, confirming and labeling each document with an exhibit number, imposing order on the hundreds and hundreds of pages that comprise an asylum claim. He invited any oral amendments to the claim, and Rosy's attorney responded with several, including a correction to a typo (clerical errors can follow asylum seekers forever, creating problems that can unravel a case) on page 56. She also requested the addition of six categories on the basis of which the asylum claim would be made. These included Rosy's identities as a single mom with children, a female business owner, a woman who defies gender norms, and a widow, as well as a couple of other categories that combined these identities, forming their own distinct categories.

The predictable preliminaries of an asylum claim ended here, with the judge advising against frivolous asylum claims, explaining what that means, and the consequences of making such claims. The rote front matter of the hearing then yielded to Rosy's testimony. It is this part of the hearing during which the unique details and variables of a person's life—most of them horribly painful—distinguish one asylum hearing from another. It is also when a government attorney or immigration judge can begin to pick apart an asylum seeker's story, wittingly or unwittingly causing anxiety and confusion with their lines of questioning, and with their own lack of knowledge and understanding about the countries and cultures from which asylum seekers come.

———

Unlike many asylum seekers, whose pro bono attorneys have limited time to meet with and ready their clients specifically for the asylum hearing, Rosy had the benefit of being prepared. Her attorney had met with her multiple times in the weeks leading up to the hearing, with the express purpose of conducting mock hearings. She even brought in another attorney to play the role of the DHS lawyer, allowing her to be as antagonistic as possible, anticipating a variety of scenarios and lines of questioning that could destabilize Rosy and shake her confidence.

The practice sessions had been extremely helpful, Rosy felt, but she told me before the hearing that she was still worried about the all-important time line. She had never been good with dates, and she knew that the "make or break" aspect of most asylum hearings involved the respondent being able to establish their credibility, in part by being able to recall the specific dates on which key events happened. Understanding Rosy's difficulty with temporal recall, her attorney responded accordingly. First, her overall strategy involved asking Rosy short, specific questions. Second, she asked Rosy's therapist to be present as a potential witness. If the DHS attorney intended to attack Rosy's credibility because of her difficulty with date recall, her attorney would call the therapist to the stand and ask questions that guided him to speak to the impact of trauma on the ability to recall dates.

Rosy's attorney asked her nearly one hundred and fifty questions, few of them longer than six words. They ranged from the standard queries of every case—What is your name? What is your date of birth? Where were you born?—to those whose answers would serve to sketch the time line and arc of the particular horrors that prompted Rosy's two perilous journeys to the United States—Where is Juan [her husband] now? Who killed him? How did he die? How did you find out? Did police investigate? How do you know they never investigated? And later, Who tried to kill you? Where were you shot? Describe your injuries. What did the hospital do for you? Do you still have a metal plate in your arm? Are your scars still visible? Could you please show the court your scars?

In response to this last question, Rosy lifted both arms, pulled her sleeves up to her elbows, and raised both forearms for the judge's inspection. "Let the record show that each of the respondent's forearms bears scars," he said.

Rosy recounted her efforts to mitigate the actual and possible harm that hung over her family in Guatemala. This is key: the respondent needs to demonstrate that they tried to actively do something to prevent the violence they experienced or, failing that, tried to go through the "proper" channels of reporting that violence and pursuing justice. Many asylum seekers never used those "proper" channels. They know firsthand what international monitoring groups report: that corruption is so deeply entrenched in institutions in Central America that average citizens, especially those who are poor, know that police and judicial authorities often act in collusion with criminals, and that justice is, at best, elusive. In Guatemala, specifically, corruption is so pervasive that over the past decade, Supreme Court judges and multiple presidents have all been indicted for corruption charges.

"Did you report your shooting to the police?" Rosy's attorney asked.

"Yes."

"Did police investigate?"

"Yes."

"What evidence did they find?"

"One bullet casing."

"Did you ever hear from police again?"

"No."

"Did you follow up with them?"

"Yes."

"What happened?"

"They said that I would have to pay them a large amount of money to carry the investigation forward."

———

Any question could have led to a lengthy story. I'd sat with Rosy and asked similar questions, and her answers could, at times, take an hour or longer. But an asylum hearing, if it is to have any hope of being successful, must excise thousands of details, especially the ones that provide context, the ones that mean the most to the person whose fate is being decided.

Less is more, effective attorneys instruct their clients. Never offer more than what you're being asked, they say. Even the judge reinforced the value of a lean narrative. In his opening instructions, he said, "Answer yes or no. If you don't know, say you don't know. If you don't understand the question, ask for it to be repeated."

———

Nearly ninety minutes after she started her questioning, Rosy's attorney indicated that she had no further questions. After a ten-minute break, the hearing resumed. It was time for the DHS attorney to attempt to chip away at Rosy's credibility and the testimony she had provided.

I took a deep breath, my stomach in a knot. What had the attorney heard and what had he not heard . . . or not listened to? During Rosy's attorney's questioning, one of our volunteers, who was seated behind the government attorney, texted me to say that the disheveled attorney was reading the CliffsNotes study guide for Charles Dickens's *Great Expectations* on his laptop.

"Please tell me you're kidding," I replied, wondering whether the attorney was consulting the CliffsNotes in some sort of preliminary effort to devise his closing statement and include a bizarre, incongruent reference to the British classic. *What must his life be like outside the courtroom?*, I wondered, as he launched into his line of questioning.

Many of his queries were redundant, possibly trying to catch inconsistencies:

After you were shot, you went to the police?

Why didn't they pursue your case?

What do you mean by "enough money for the investigation"?

One has to put forth *money* to get action?

Remarkably, he ended after a couple dozen questions, and even declined to offer a closing statement. Was his mojo low, or was he just convinced enough by her testimony that he felt no need to try to wrest a denial from this case? I was puzzled and a bit unsettled. What would happen next?

———

Typically, the conclusion of an asylum hearing can take one of two paths. A judge may decide to issue a written asylum decision via mail because he or she wants more time to review the case file and consider the testimony alongside it. The other possibility is that the judge will issue a same-day oral decision, particularly if the facts of the case are strong, whether for or against the asylum claim.

In Rosy's case, neither happened.

The judge, in his concluding remarks, revealed the reason for the earlier sidebar: a key piece of information was missing from Rosy's file. Without it, he couldn't make a final determination in her case. Though her attorney had requested biometrics—the fingerprinting and background check required to accompany asylum cases—nearly a year earlier, the government had never given her the appointment to have these performed. The government attorney had offered Rosy the chance to defer the hearing until her biometrics were complete or have the hearing, with the understanding that the judge could not make a ruling until he had the opportunity to review the results. She chose the latter. Assuming that the government will give her an appointment and that the results will come in time—a fairly generous assumption given its record—her next hearing, the *final* final hearing, will be held in February 2020.

————

Although there was no decision in the case, Rosy was still in good spirits when we left the courtroom. The most difficult step in the asylum process was over, and she felt good about it all: her attorney's efficacy, her own performance (she had cried, briefly, only once, and had been calm and collected throughout the questioning), the DHS attorney's tepid demeanor, the support she had from friends and volunteers, and the judge's attitude, which she perceived to be fair.

We all piled into the car and headed to dinner. It was still drizzling, but the rain was letting up and the clouds were clearing, with stars stippling the sky. It wasn't a celebration—not yet—but we treated it like one anyway, ordering a dozen oysters to share. Plump, briny, fresh, we each took an oyster and held it up as if to toast. While we didn't have a decision, we'd all done all we could to make Rosy's case. We had a wait ahead. But tonight? Tonight, we'd celebrate. We would honor Rosy. Her grit. Her love for her children. Her survival. Her ability, after all she had lived through and overcome, to keep opening up herself to a life of possibility, one of dreams that—we all felt even if we didn't say it—seemed ever closer within reach.

Rosy was granted asylum on February 4, 2020. The judge's decision also meant that Yordy and Fernando could remain in the United States legally. Rosy is now in the process of filing for legal status for her daughters.

Recommended Reading

Over the years, I've read a number of books that have shaped my thinking about Latin America, social justice, and social change. What follows is by no means a comprehensive list, but they are the texts that I have returned to time and again since starting what has become Immigrant Families Together. I commend them to you in the hope that you will find them as informative and inspiring and thought-provoking as I have.

—Julie

The Guatemala Reader: History, Culture, Politics. Edited by Greg Grandin, Deborah T. Levenson, and Elizabeth Oglesby. Duke University Press, 2011.

This anthology, one title in the press's Latin America Readers series, offers a broad and deep introduction to Guatemalan history, drawing on primary source writings that cover a sweeping period, from the precolonial era to the first decade of the twenty-first century. People looking to fill gaps in their knowledge and to gain context about some of the root causes of the migration "crisis" would do well to delve into this hefty volume.

A Burst of Light and Other Essays. Audre Lorde. Ixia Press, 2017.

I was introduced to Audre Lorde's work in my college women's studies classes. Her most widely known idea is a powerfully articulated one: "The master's tools will never dismantle the master's house." But it's an idea that I could never understand fully until many years later when I was deep in the work I'm committed to now. In this book, Lorde, who wrote many of the essays as she was facing death from cancer, reflects upon her years of intersectional activism and upon the powers of fear, longing, rage, and silence. I have easily underlined half of the lines in this book.

Vanishing Frontiers: The Forces Driving Mexico and the United States Together. Andrew Selee. PublicAffairs, 2018.

Even as a former resident of Mexico and a devoted Mexiphile, I learned immense amounts about borders—and the Mexico-US border in particular—from Andrew Selee's smart book, which draws from his experiences working for decades in the field of migration policy. The joy of this book is that it's neither inaccessibly wonky nor a doom-and-gloom tale. Instead, it makes its case for a future in which borders are less rigid and more permeable by detailing numerous success stories that tend to escape media attention but prove the promise and possibility of cross-border collaborations.

Barking to the Choir: The Power of Radical Kinship. Gregory Boyle. Simon & Schuster, 2017.

This book by Jesuit priest Gregory Boyle, founder of the Los Angeles–based social service program Homeboy Industries, is a compendium of feel-good anecdotes from his years of work with active and former gang members. By rooting his life and his work in the notion of radical kinship—the idea that we are all responsible for one another and that we should "stand in awe at what folks have to carry rather than in judgment at how they carry it"—Father Greg has touched thousands of lives in his three decades of ministry and activism.

How to Get Involved

"How can I help?"

If that's the question you're asking yourself after reading this book, here are a few answers—ways for you to get involved in supporting asylum seekers and other immigrant neighbors.

1. **Read.** Learning more about the history of immigration and migration, borders, and the complicated relationships between the United States and other countries is crucial to understanding the root causes of migration and immigration policies. Reading about these subjects will help fill in the vital context often absent from mainstream media news reports.

2. **Be politically aware and active.** Voting is an essential act, of course, but writing and calling elected officials to support or express opposition to policies that harm migrants and the diversity of our communities are other ways to exercise your rights. Pay attention to local politics, too, even at the municipal level. Local and state policies, such as allowing municipal police to collaborate with ICE, often prop up federal poli-

cies or, in ideal scenarios, propose alternatives that advance a more progressive agenda.

3. **Use the power of the purse.** Where you shop and what you buy matter. Avoid patronizing companies that support detention centers and their contractors. The website and app Goods Unite Us (www.goodsuniteus.com) evaluates and scores companies based on their political donations, allowing you to direct your dollars in a way that's aligned with your own beliefs.

4. **Donate.** Organizations dedicated to migration and borderlands issues use your contributions to provide direct support to asylum seekers. Donations to Immigrant Families Together (www.immigrantfamiliestogether.com) pay for asylum seekers' bonds and cover the expenses for their legal fees, housing, food, health care, and transportation to and from legal appointments. This level of support provides families with greater safety and stability while they are waiting for their asylum decision, as the majority of them are not yet allowed to work. If you don't have money to donate, host a fundraiser! A lemonade stand can raise enough money to feed a family—there's no such thing as "too small" or "too little."

5. **Volunteer.** While many organizations doing the day-to-day work of supporting asylum seekers simply don't have the

staffing to be able to manage volunteers, others rely on people who can volunteer their time and energy to the organization's work. One of these is Team Brownsville (www .teambrownsville.org), in Brownsville, Texas, which feeds asylum seekers and welcomes them at the local bus station upon their release from detention. They are always looking for volunteers to help serve meals.

6. **Get crafty.** A number of special arts and crafts projects invite you to use your talent and skill to show solidarity with asylum seekers and other immigrants. One particularly lovely project is Welcome Blanket (www.welcomeblanket.org), which invites quilters and knitters to make blankets that "provide literal and symbolic comfort and warmth" for people who have newly arrived in the United States.

Acknowledgments—Rosy

First, my profound gratitude goes to God for allowing this project to be realized. I also thank each one of the people who has become part of my life since I was released from Eloy, those who have been essential to my stay in this country. There are many of them, and I mention only a few here, though I am thankful for every one of them:

To Julie—thank you for taking the initiative to support the mothers who are separated from their children. I know that all you've been through hasn't been easy, and yet you continue to persist in this grand work. Thank you to your husband, Francisco, for his unconditional support and, of course, to each one of your children. Together, you make an incredible team that's been able to reunite many families.

To Bonnie and your family—I give my thanks for all of the moral support that you've offered us—thank you for making us feel like your family.

To Vicky—what could I possibly say? There are so many things, but above all, I thank you for making space for me in your life, not just by opening the door to your home but also the door to your heart. The love that you feel for us is what we feel for you as well, and no matter where we go, you will always be in our hearts. Thanks also to your sons for making us feel at home.

To Rabbi Rachel Timoner and each and every one of the people from Congregation Beth Elohim who in one way or another supported us when we lived in Brooklyn—thank you for your visits and for not leaving us alone at the time when we needed you so much.

To Monique—thank you for opening your home to us, entrusting it to us, and allowing us to stay there in what was such a time of need for us.

To Hannah—thank you for always thinking of us and providing support in the most important moments of our process.

To my sons—thank you for your patience and for understanding each moment that we've lived. Thank you for accompanying me in this process.

To my daughters—I have so much love for you, and it hurts me that you are not at my side, but you are always in my heart. Thank you for being so strong. I know that our Creator will continue to strengthen your hearts and allow you to grow and to keep going.

To my guide and great warrior woman, my beautiful mother—I love and miss you. Thank you for being my pillar.

To my sister Elvira and her family—thank you for your unconditional support in caring for my daughters while we go through this process.

To the rest of my family—I love you and I give thanks for each one of you. All of you have been and will always be an essential part of my daily life. May God bless you always.

To Scott—thank you for your faith in this book, and to HarperOne, thank you for caring about this important issue, a side of life that people don't often see.

Finally, thank you to everyone who is a part of my daily life and to each one of you who is holding this book in your hands and reading my story.

Acknowledgments—Julie

I started my professional life as a social worker and creative arts therapist who specialized in using writing as a way of helping people tell their life stories—and as a way of helping them imagine, work toward, and, ultimately, realize a different, hopefully happier, ending. I left that career behind in 2003. I loved my work and the people I was doing it with and for, but I was deeply frustrated by organizational bureaucracy. I shelved my vision of changing the world, or my little corner of it, through social work and instead became a writer, editor, and translator, still telling stories, mostly about Latin America.

In a strange and wonderful way, then, my life has come full circle. At its heart, the work of Immigrant Families Together is about telling stories, about being the voice for people who don't have the chance to take the microphone or bullhorn and tell their own narratives. In this book, I am both grateful and proud to help tell Rosy's story, but also, to give her the bullhorn. Her story is just that—uniquely hers—but its basic contours represent the stories of thousands of Central Americans seeking refuge in the United States. She—and they—along with her children are people you would be glad to have as your neighbors, people who remind us of why this country was founded and what the American dream really is.

I am grateful to our agent, Scott Mendel, who called to say, "You know you need to put together a book proposal, right?" and who helped shape that proposal and kept it moving forward so that Rosy's story—which, in many ways, is the story of all IFT moms and families—could gain the greatest visibility and the largest audience, inviting, we hope, a reset on our national conversation about immigration. Every writer should be so lucky to have him in their corner.

I am grateful, also, to the HarperOne team, Shannon Welch, Edward Benitez, and Judith Curr, who believed in the importance of Rosy's story, so much so that they made the decision to publish the book in English and Spanish simultaneously. The fact that *The Book of Rosy* can reach readers in both languages means a great deal to Rosy and to myself.

This book wouldn't be possible, of course, without the volunteers of Immigrant Families Together, both the one-time donors who understood in the deepest fibers of their beings that, yes, they *could* make a difference—even the woman who sent the last $3 from her Social Security check, apologizing that she couldn't send more—and those who have been all-in from day one or early on, including Cathey Ambush, Evelyn Belasco, Jessica Berg, Kelly Carter, Amelie Cherlin, Micaela Coiro, Stephanie Diehl, Sara Farrington, Meghan Finn, Jonathan Forgash, Karina Franco, Gina Katz, Rosalie Lochner, Jenn Morson, Sara

Nolan, Casey Revkin Ryan, Megan Stotts, Courtney Sullivan, Laurie Sweet, Zoë Van Tieghem, Allyson Vaughn, and Emily Spokes Warren. Your partners and children deserve so much of my gratitude, too, having shared you and your precious time with families who need you as much, if not more, than your own families need you. Some of us still haven't met "in real life," but I'd walk through fire for you or with you. I have no doubt forgotten someone who has been vital to our work, and if you are that person, I beg your apologies.

Beyond the core volunteers, there are many—hundreds—more who have played an ongoing role, including drivers and hosts, regional support teams, organizational partners and pro bono providers, and the astonishing number of you who have done the real grunt work, day in and day out, beyond the sight of any camera lens or reporter's microphone. There are too many of you to name and I ask your forgiveness if I haven't acknowledged you here, but I would be particularly remiss not to mention Rabbi Stephanie Kolin; Rabbi Rachel Timoner and Congregation Beth Elohim and its Refugee Task Force; the Reform Temple of Forest Hills; Temple Tikvah of New Hyde Park; Miles4Migrants; Catholic Charities of New York; RAICES; the Southern Poverty Law Center; the International Rescue Committee; Sergio Cordova and Michael Benavides of Team Brownsville; Juan Ortiz and Jen Apodaca in El Paso, Texas; Tribeca Pediatrics; the NYU Dental Clinic; and the Lumos Foundation.

I am grateful beyond measure to the journalists who have borne the unrelenting brunt of covering the Trump Administration's innumerable abuses, but especially the ones related to immigration. If there's a heaven, and Rosy assures me there is, then a special corner is reserved there for the many reporters who have covered this beat from the beginning, and who have done so sensitively, treating families with the respect and care they need and deserve while bringing their stories to a wider audience: Beth Fertig of WNYC; Annie Correal, Nick Kristof, and photographer Tamir Kalifa of the *New York Times*; Emily Kinskey of *TIME* magazine; Josh Robin of NY1; Pablo Gutierrez of Univisión; Pamela Larson of *Arizona Central* and *USA Today*; Christina Tkacik of the *Baltimore Sun*; and so many more, including freelancer Sandi Bachom, who shot the viral video of Yeni for NowThis, and my dear friend Alice Driver, a freelance journalist who, over the past year, has reported on the borderlands and current migration dynamics for CNN, Longreads, *National Geographic*, *TIME*, and *Reveal*, among other outlets. If there is one single thing that has continuously helped move the needle in terms of public pressure and policy changes, it is persistent media coverage that has not let zero tolerance and the Trump Administration's other cruel, inept immigration policies fall out of the public eye. Your work is hard. It is also crucial. Keep it up.

Of course, I feel like my life will always be at least loosely entwined with that of José Orochena, both of us having stumbled into the zero-tolerance arena, our lives forever changed by it. José and the other attorneys and their staff members who represent or assist IFT families in their asylum cases are the overlooked, unsung heroes of the zero-tolerance story. Among them are people who I now count as friends and *compañeros* and *compañeras en la lucha*. Chief among them are Ray Ybarra Maldonado, Angeles Maldonado, and Mana Yegani.

Without the support of Senator Michael Gianaris, Congressman Adriano Espaillat, New York Attorney General Letitia James, Assemblywoman Aravella Simotas, Congresswoman Carolyn Maloney, Congresswoman Alexandria Ocasio-Cortez, and Senator Cory Booker, I feel certain we wouldn't have been able to reunify families as quickly as we have nor gain the visibility and traction we needed to begin affecting policy at a bigger-picture level. You are all true leaders who walk the walk.

To Kristen Bell, Molly McNearney, several anonymous donors who made large recurring donations, the Hispanic Federation, and the Lumos Foundation: you allowed us to scale when I was terrified but determined to do so. Your ongoing support is meaningful beyond measure, and every day I wake up still astonished by your generosity and grateful for your trust.

I wouldn't have been able to help write this book, much less do any of the work described between its covers, without the support and tolerance of my family. From my first "I have a wild idea" declaration to days spent at immigration and nights spent at bus stations or hospitals or airports, and hours upon hours spent on the phone, Francisco and our kids have sacrificed so much of their own lives, opening themselves up to share with others ourselves and our home and everything we have. It is my greatest hope that I have helped repay some of the debt owed to the family who took Francisco in nearly forty years ago and that I have helped our children understand that our great privilege makes *hineini* the only answer that's worth articulating.

In February 2019, I traveled to Guatemala to meet Rosy's family and was welcomed like a daughter and a sister by her mother, Doña Fernanda; her sister Elvira; her brother-in-law Edgar; their children; Rosy's daughters; and Rosy's other siblings. Elvira and Edgar went out of their way to take care of me and answer my hundreds of questions and satisfy my many curiosities, as did Doña Fernanda, who also shared her tequila with me generously, fed me her home-cooked tacos and rice tamales, and taught me all about the local hooch, *machetero*. I know that my first visit won't be the last one, and I am conscious that Rosy's story is their story, too. It is my greatest hope that I have helped tell their story in a way that honors them.

Finally, my life is absolutely and forever changed by Rosy, Yordy, and Fernando and the (as of this writing) 106 other parents, grandparents, and siblings we have reunited with younger children; we support more than 106 families. Collectively, you have taught me the true meaning of strength and resilience, of faith, family, and what it means to strive for a better future. I am honored and humbled to play a small part in your life stories, and my life is enriched irrevocably by our bonds. Know that I am your biggest fan, standing on the sidelines and cheering you on, and that no matter the outcome, I will be here for you.